MW01122851

The Romance of Libraries

Edited by
Madeleine Lefebvre

The Scarecrow Press, Inc.
Lanham, Maryland • Toronto • Oxford
2006

SCARECROW PRESS, INC.

Published in the United States of America
by Scarecrow Press, Inc.
A wholly owned subsidiary of
The Rowman & Littlefield Publishing Group, Inc.
4501 Forbes Boulevard, Suite 200, Lanham, Maryland 20706
www.scarecrowpress.com

PO Box 317
Oxford
OX2 9RU, UK

Copyright © 2006 by Madeleine Lefebvre

All *rights reserved*. No part of this publication may be reproduced,
stored in a retrieval system, or transmitted in any form or by any
means, electronic, mechanical, photocopying, recording, or otherwise,
without the prior permission of the publisher.

British Library Cataloguing in Publication Information Available

Library of Congress Cataloging-in-Publication Data

The romance of libraries / edited by Madeleine Lefebvre.
  p.   cm.
  ISBN 0-8108-5352-3 (pbk. : alk. paper)
  1. Libraries—Humor. 2. Libraries—Anecdotes.   I. Lefebvre, Madeleine,
1951–

  Z682.5.R66   2005
  027—dc22   2005018779

♾ ™ The paper used in this publication meets the minimum requirements of
American National Standard for Information Sciences—Permanence of Paper
for Printed Library Materials, ANSI/NISO Z39.48–1992. Manufactured in the
United States of America.

In memory of my parents,
who first gave me a love of libraries and reading,
and my grandmother,
who passed on her love of writing.

Contents

~

Foreword

Most people do not know how greatly love and libraries are entwined, but the estimable Jimmy Buffett, the bard of rum and romance, knows the power to sway the human heart of libraries and the works they contain. As he tells us in his song "Love in the Library," strange things happen to those "surrounded by stories, surreal and sublime." The air of libraries is charged with mystery and the sense of possibilities—the bespectacled man in the corner reading quietly may be a Clark Kent and the music librarian's unobtrusive efficiency may be merely the public face of a volcanic private life. One of the primary unacknowledged purposes of a university library is to be a meeting place for students with more on their mind than cramming for classes. Has there ever been a coming-of-age novel set on a university campus that did not contain a description of a tryst in the library? Public libraries are where smart teenagers go to learn about love and life from books when they tire of the lonely aridities of the Internet—they are, therefore, the perfect place for smart teenagers to meet others whose intellect matches theirs. If Charlie Brown did not meet the cute redheaded girl in his school library, he should have. What better site could there be for the first encounter in that saddest of all modern unrequited love stories? I know of romances that have bloomed in the Library of Congress and the late lamented British Museum Reading Room. I also know a sad tale of love thwarted and a lover stranded in a small suburban public branch library. You see, libraries great and small have the power to inspire and fan the flame of love triumphant and love denied. They are full of stories—romances (tales of adventures, surprising incident, love, etc.)[1]—and expressions of the human heart from music to movies and beyond. They are peopled by bookish people, music lovers, film buffs, and all the other members of the great nation within nations that comprises all those to whom the human heart and its mysteries are the central question of life. Why else are Dickens, Mozart, and John Ford important? Where can you tap in to the magic of their dreams better and more easily than in libraries? Is it any wonder that a library of any size is charged with emotion and, therefore, human beings who are sensitive to the power of the emanations of the human spirit should find libraries places of love and romance in all their complexities and profundity?

That is what this book explores and delineates, the understanding that the library is a place that, like the moon, makes men and women especially open to the urgings of the heart that are far stronger than any other force when they come to us. These stories of love in all its many forms and manifestations all speak to that power as much as they do to the ever-fascinating twists and turns of love. We should be grateful to Madeleine Lefebvre because she thought of this book and to the many who have told her their tales of their library loves. Chance encounters lead to long happy marriages; determined wooings lead to disaster and loss (though even those stories are testaments to the fact that it is better to have loved and lost than never to have loved at all)[2]; and happy encounters leading to nowhere much are looked back on with fondness. Jimmy Buffett understands all these because he too has known love in the library, entranced by a young woman who sent him "a smile as she reached for Flaubert." Perhaps it was Emma Bovary for which she was reaching—a love story that ends very badly—but it was a magic moment for all that.

Enjoy this book and never underestimate the power of a library to change lives, not least by allowing romance to flourish.

Michael Gorman

Notes

1. As *Webster's New Collegial Dictionary* tells us.
2. A phrase attributed to Samuel Butler and to Alfred, Lord Tennyson.

~

Acknowledgments

I must first thank all the people who contacted me, keen to tell the story of their romance and the role that libraries have played in their lives. Without their contributions there would be no book. Thanks are due, too, to the people who directed me toward stories. In particular, my thanks go to the following contributors who crafted longer submissions: Theresa and Curtis Babiar; Jason Bird; Nancy Black; Barb Carr; The Reverend Dr. Michael J. J. Collier; Rodney Eloy and Marcia Regina; John J. Heney; Nina Leibfacher; Margy MacMillan (for her recipe); Mike Madigan; Dorothy McEown; Maria Coletta McLean; Prapti Mehta; Jill Kempshall; Carrie Ann Smith; Simon Smith; Margaret Stafford; George and Nancy Stewart; and John Tate. Unfortunately there are others I cannot name to protect their privacy, but I thank them too.

Michael Gorman's writing on library values has been a major inspiration. I am indebted to him for being gracious enough to write the foreword. I would also like to thank all my library colleagues who have been so encouraging; especially the librarians and staff of the Patrick Power Library of Saint Mary's University. Doug Vaisey was a big help in tracking down elusive references, and Victoria Sigurdson designed a lovely website from my vague ideas. Bill Richardson, Heather Kennedy, and Heidi Petracek of CBC Radio were very helpful in promoting the project. CBC's *Richardson's Roundup* launched a contest to help gather stories to get me off to a good start.

A special thank-you goes to Dalhousie University Professor Emeritus

Norman Horrocks for all his good advice and encouragement, not just with this project but in my daily working life.

Finally, huge and heartfelt thanks must go to Angela Dinaut and Larry Lefebvre for their expertise and patience with the manuscript. Their feedback and support has been invaluable.

CHAPTER ONE

Dear Library . . .

I've had a romance with libraries since I was a small child. It's not just the contents that attract me, it's the whole package—the building, the atmosphere, the people who work in them, and the people who use them. So many stories sit on the shelves and so many more unfold daily on the floor. Like many librarians, I always try to locate the local library when I'm traveling somewhere new, and usually take a photograph. The snapshot of the library is like a snapshot of the locale and its personality. While magnificent architectural masterpieces have been constructed over the years and are still being built, the small Carnegie libraries, discovered by chance, often have the most romantic atmospheres. The fact that they were created due to the generosity and forethought of a philanthropist adds to their cachet. Andrew Carnegie was motivated by the belief that libraries were the means to allow any member of society to educate themselves and build on their own strengths to their fullest potential.[1] (I'd like to think he had sentimental reasons as well: Did Andrew Carnegie find love in a library?)

Nevertheless there are many large and famous libraries that also spark the romantic imagination. I recently revisited the magnificent circular Reading Room in the British Museum. Winter sunlight was streaming through the windows under its dome. I stood for a few moments in reverie, wondering how many romances, both overt and covert, had been kindled there. The Reading Room has a palpable atmosphere—like a living, breathing entity. It also has excellent acoustics; before long, the quiet conversation between two desk attendants broke through my thoughts. They were discussing one's forthcoming redundancy package, and the unexpected benefit he was about to receive of a free bus pass to search for another job. Clearly they were immune to the romance of the Reading Room, or perhaps the anxieties of their working lives had relegated romantic notions solely to awestruck visitors.

My father ran a branch library for a regional system for many years. Throughout my school education, I regularly accompanied him to the library. I would sit on the floor in my favorite corner, reading the books within easy reach along the bottom shelves. There was another smaller branch within walking distance of our home. I was a frequent user of that library as well.

I have very happy memories of the time I spent in my father's library. I would go there after school and go home with him when the library closed. On school vacations I often spent entire days there, shelving books and filing cards. Elderly ladies would come in for the latest romance or mystery and compliment my dad for "having his little helper today." On his breaks Dad would put his feet up in the staff room and dive back into whatever book he was currently reading, and I would do the same. I had the sense that reading was his primary occupation—punctuated by necessary breaks to go back to work. It felt companionable, comforting, and safe. It's not surprising then that I eventually became a librarian. For me, libraries will always be places of personal growth, companionship, sociability, service, security, peace, and knowledge. I was to realize later that they are also places of romance.

The library as the setting for romance has been repeatedly explored in literature. A personal favorite is Tom Stoppard's play *Travesties*. Set in the Zurich Public Library during World War I it involves, in one of its many intricate plots, a romance between a British consular official and a beautiful librarian named Cecily. James Joyce, Lenin, and Dadaist Tristan Tzara also frequent the library to provide commentary.

Websites have been devoted to romantic fiction set in libraries,[2] and librarian protagonists in film and television.[3] I share Michael Gorman's view of *Desk Set* as "the definitive 'information science' movie."[4] How could Spencer Tracy fail to fall in love with such a smart and sassy librarian as Katherine Hepburn?

After listening to many keynote speeches at conferences I realized that most people have a cherished personal story that is connected with a library. While it's a given for those of us in the profession, it is noticeable that others outside the field, when addressing library conferences, will begin with fond tales of favorite librarians, childhood memories of the library, and sometimes more personal stories of romance. It made me wonder. If I was regularly hearing stories of deep emotional connections with libraries, could there be many more? If so, could the imminent demise of the physical library—as expounded by the naysayers and doom forecasters in professional literature and on occasion in the mainstream media—be a genuine threat, or is the physical library so embedded in the emotional psyche that society won't let that happen?

As soon as I began talking about romance in libraries, the idea generated interest. I did some research to see if this topic had been addressed before in fact, as opposed to fiction. When Paul Wiener of the State University of New York–Stony Brook advertised in the October 1985 issue of *American Libraries* his plan to conduct a survey of librarian couples, he received an enthusiastic response. Almost a hundred couples responded to his survey, while almost two hundred sent photographs of themselves to the magazine.[5]

I wanted to take a wider view that wasn't just limited to librarian couples. I started a website, www.libraryromance.com, to see if the virtual world would help me locate stories. Very quickly the website was getting hits and being picked up on blogs. I put out a call through electronic discussion lists and alumni groups, and wrote to newspapers and magazines. I advertised the project at conferences.

I had assumed at first that the stories would all be based in North America, but before long they were coming in from all over the world. I was fascinated by all the different voices I heard in the narratives. Regardless of location and circumstances, these voices were unified in their emotional response to libraries. Themes and patterns emerged. In every case a library (or a library-related setting) played a role in the story, almost like a character itself.

While the common message is the same, each story is different. By letting the stories speak for themselves I hope that what emerges is a multifaceted love letter to libraries and the value they bring to our lives.

It isn't surprising that in some instances, couples were too shy or private to have their story appear in print. Many others, however, were only too happy to share their joy. Another group was willing to have their story included but asked for anonymity of name and place. A small number of stories fell into the "lust in the stacks" category. I debated whether to include them. Passion is certainly an element of romance, but there was a sense of calculation and planning about them—as though conducting the relationship in the library was part of the thrill—that didn't fit well with the theme of this book. It was noticeable too that these relationships were relatively short-lived, whereas many of the romances outlined in the book have lasted for many years. In the stories I've included there is a sense of a romantic force at work that brought the couple together and kept them together. I'd like to think that this force came from the library itself.

Contributors wrote most of the stories in e-mails to me. Prompted on my website, several included song titles that were special to them. I edited the narratives as little as possible to allow them to be told in their own words. Using e-mail as a medium encouraged many storytellers to be less formal and their emotions more immediate. I have tempered that intimacy by supplying only their first names, and pseudonyms when requested. New Mexican author Rudolfo Anaya says

I am an oral storyteller, but now I do it on the printed page.[6]

I wanted to convey that sense of oral storytelling in this book because I am a firm believer in the power of stories to teach us about ourselves and others. I once read on a wall "I don't know what I think until I hear what I say."

Some contributors chose to craft longer stories with titles. I have honored their titles and included their full names. A few stories I gathered from previously published sources. Others came from interviews or personal knowledge and were written by me. I know there must be many more stories not in this book. If you have one you would like to share, please visit www.libraryromance.com and let me know. I plan to continue collecting stories as long as people want to send them to me.

This project truly has been a labor of love. I feel I have gotten to know something about the contributors through their submissions:

their happiness, sadness, and overall thankfulness for what libraries have brought into their lives. Some have even sent me photographs commemorating their milestones. I have gained a new group of friends of all ages. (One contributor is ninety-seven years old!)

I called this book *The Romance of Libraries* because it's not just about people finding romance with each other at the library. It's about the attraction that libraries and their values have for us. Many of us fall in love in libraries, it seems, because we have already fallen in love *with* libraries.

Now open the door, step into a familiar world, and enjoy these endearing stories that I hope will soften even the most unromantic heart.

Notes

1. Michael Lorenzen, "Deconstructing the Philanthropic Library: The Sociological Reasons behind Andrew Carnegie's Millions to Libraries," *Illinois Libraries* 81, no. 2 (Spring 1999): 75.

2. See www.jenw.org/home.htm, for example.

3. See http://emp.byui.edu/raishm/films/introduction.html, for example.

4. Michael Gorman, *Our Enduring Values* (Chicago and London: American Library Association, 2000), dedication.

5. Paul Benjamin Wiener, "Marryin' the Librarian: Two-Librarian Marriages Get 'Thumbs-up' from Survey Respondents," *American Libraries* 17, no.1 (January 1986): 16–23.

6. Rudolfo Anaya, www.unm.edu/~wrtgsw/anaya.html (accessed January 5, 2005).

CHAPTER TWO

The Library as Place—of Romance

Some famous couples reportedly met in the library. Former U.S. President Bill Clinton and Senator Hillary Rodham Clinton had seen each other around the Yale campus, but first spoke to each other in the Yale Law Library. They had been aware of each other, even staring at each other. Hillary took the initiative and strode up to Bill to introduce herself in a very direct way, rendering Bill temporarily speechless, as he recalls in his autobiography.[1] Hillary also refers to their meeting in the library in her autobiography.[2] Laura Orr followed up on that meeting.

> I worked as a reference librarian at the Yale Law Library from 1991–2000 and during the Clinton-Gore presidential campaign of 1992, I wrote to Bill Clinton asking if it was true that he and Hillary met in the Yale Law Library and if he could say where. I included in my letter a map of the Yale Law Library Reading Room, which was where it was said they first met. I got back from then-candidate Clinton a marvelous and very funny letter. I of course posted it in the Yale Law Library and am periodically asked about it by former co-workers.[3]

It is reported in many sources that prolific author Stephen King met his wife, Tabitha Spruce, when they were both working at the Fogler Library of the University of Maine. Noted children's author and poet Jack Prelutsky met his wife Carolynn in the children's room in the Albuquerque Public Library in October 1979. According to Carolynn, Jack proposed to her ten minutes after they met, and they were married that December.[4]

In recognition of their place in a romantic couple's affections, libraries have often been chosen to witness their special occasions. Proposals, engagements, weddings, and special anniversaries have all been celebrated in libraries. The University of Illinois at Urbana-Champaign reported

Feelings have always run deep for the Library, so deep that tales of Library romances are legion. At least two couples have gotten married in the Library in the last 25 years.

Norman Smith and Peggy Ehrhart, who now live in Leonia, New Jersey, were graduate students pursuing their doctorates in the 1970s—he in comparative literature and she, English—when they decided to say their vows in June of 1975 in the Rare Book and Special Collections Library, Room 346 of the Library.

Rebecca Brackmann, who is working on her doctorate in English at Illinois, and her husband, Craig Steffen, who has a doctorate in physics and now works for the National Center for Supercomputing Applications, which is based at Illinois, got married in November of last year on the grand staircase of the Library, just below the circulation desk on one side, and the reference Room on the other.

Then there was the couple who affirmed their affection for each other and for the Library even more permanently. When they were graduate students, George Carlson and Lynda Tepfer had adjoining carrels in the Library, on the north wall of the stacks. In time, they fell in love and married. On their 25th wedding anniversary, they came back to the Library and had a plaque affixed to the wall of carrel 1012, 10/12 being their wedding date.

The small bronze and wood plaque reads "In recognition of George and Lynda Carlson on the occasion of their Illinois Silver Anniversary 25 years after meeting in the Library."[5]

The library as place is a hotly discussed topic, apparently even more so these days in the face of the electronic library onslaught. For several years now at the Patrick Power Library at Saint Mary's University we have been working to transform the library into a welcoming, social, and attractive gathering place for students—making it a much more congenial space. From my research for this book, however, it would appear that regardless of atmosphere, food policy, or other regulations, the university library—any university library—always has been a magnet for romantic encounters. Perhaps it's the comfortable chairs, the secluded stack areas, and the plethora of attractive students on a mission. I would like to think, though, that the contents of the books on the shelves help create the right climate for romance. Perhaps the urgent passion of an Andrew Marvell poem or the romantic encounters of the heroes and heroines of the Brontës and Jane Austen are sending subliminal impulses through the covers to create the highly charged atmosphere of the stacks.

The student psyche always knows where the hot spots are on campus for meeting a potential romantic partner.

Jennifer's Story

In September 1989, I was in my graduating year at St. Francis Xavier. As with most universities, the library was the social hot spot. Girls dressed up to go there, as if they were going out clubbing or to a party. But that's not where I saw Brad. No, I saw him on the rugby field and in the current periodicals reading room. He was reading voraciously, stacks of newspapers and journals, most not relevant to his current field of study. Soon we started dating and would often meet in front of the library after classes, head off in separate directions to study undistracted, and then meet back when the library closed to walk home. After graduation we moved to Halifax. I began work at the Killam Library (at Dalhousie University) as a science cataloger and then proceeded to attend library school there. Brad worked at a busy nightclub and so our opposite schedules didn't allow us much time together. But every day Brad would be waiting for me in, of course, the current periodicals reading room, bringing a smile to my face. We married in 1995 and headed to northern Maine, so Brad could complete a teaching degree. Now the roles were reversed and it was I who waited for Brad in the library. I would fill my days reading, volunteering, searching databases, and assisting Brad with his research. In 2004, things are very different again. I'm a librarian at Acadia University and Brad is a teacher, but you won't find either of us hanging around the university library in our free time anymore. Now we attend Tiny Tales and we aren't reading as many journal articles; rather, we are reading aloud Little Critter, Robert Munsch, and Captain Underpants at our public library. We're loving, laughing with, and reading to our two little boys, Spencer and Carter, and hoping that, either in a book or for real, they will find love at the library.

Patricia's Story

It was 1969 and the University of New South Wales Library was the "in" place for Eastern suburbs Higher School Certificate (HSC) students to hang out on weekends and after school hours doing preparation for the looming HSC trials and then the final HSC exams.

As a Bondi Junction Holy Cross College student I had regularly used the University of New South Wales Library, particularly since I lived quite close by in Randwick. The library was also a social venue for students to gather at and gossip, and of course to occasionally flirt with boys. This was the sixties and good Catholic high school girls had limited opportunities to fraternize with the opposite sex. A library setting was perfect. It was neutral ground and one rarely had any objections from a parent when the request was to go study at the library.

One weekend, I headed for the library and met up with friends. As usual we chatted about who fancied what boy, who we might spot while at the library. A close friend of mine mentioned a guy she was keen on who she thought was "so gorgeous!" He wrote her long, deep, and meaningful letters from boarding school. Maybe he'd be there. He sometimes visited to do his studying too. Later on, my friend excitedly, almost breathlessly, told me he was there. Carl was there! "Come quickly and you'll get a chance to see the gorgeous hunk," she said.

Obligingly, as a good friend would do, I followed her into the library stacks. She pointed him out between the bookshelves. Hmmm, I thought. He's okay. But not really a "gorgeous hunk!" I had to pretend he was "cute" of course and make some positive comments so her feelings wouldn't be hurt. Another friend introduced me to Carl on the steps of the library later. I liked him better then but not enough to think about him again.

The next two years were a blur of finishing up at school and leaving home for teachers' college in a country town. The library at New South Wales University seemed a remote snip out of my earlier life. Little did I know that within a couple of years, I would be the lover of this man

I first spied at a library, and shortly afterward, when he had completed his own university studies, become his wife and the mother of his children.

Almost thirty-five years later, we're still happily married. He now works in a university library and I still hold on to some fond memories of that first library liaison. He is my gorgeous hunk now at fifty-three years old! We'll live happily ever after.

Sue's Story

I first met my husband at a Manchester high school which had separate buildings for boys and girls. The only mixed department was the library where I used to go with my friends at recess. He was with a group of boys who used to come into the library to whisper and tease us girls. He was taller, broader, and blonder than the rest, but I noticed him because he was the quiet one.

We've been married for twenty-nine years now and have two big, broad, blond sons. My husband was diagnosed with cancer four years ago, so I don't know how many more years we'll have together. Our special song is Art Garfunkel's "I Only Have Eyes for You."

Darren's Story

My partner and I met at the Vancouver Public Library in British Columbia five years ago. We didn't meet in the stacks or checkout line. We met in the basement on a makeshift dance floor with a few hundred other folks celebrating Gay Pride weekend. Talk about creating a space for the community to meet! The lucky part is that we both lived in Seattle and had found each other in an unlikely spot in another country.

Five years have gone by and the library is a regular part of our anniversary visits to Vancouver. It's especially fitting for me because I'm also a librarian. So my professional and personal loves have combined in a way I'd never thought possible. There's even some discussion about getting married at Vancouver Public Library under their grand coliseum archways.

Sarah's Story

He's a friendly fellow who converses happily with anyone sharing his interests—it just happened to be me each Thursday evening at my solitary post behind the desk of the children's department desk in the basement of the Streetsville, Ontario, library.

I eventually moved on, taking promotions to other branches in the Mississauga Library System and didn't see Gordon over the next few years except for a few brief chance meetings at malls and movies and once when he happened to visit one of the branches where I was working.

I continued for several years to move up, at last landing in another basement, this one at the large central library where the bookmobile offices were hidden. Unknown to me, Gordon would (and still does) spend many midday hours there, researching and writing books and reviews between driving his bus routes. We inevitably rekindled our acquaintance late in the summer of 2001 and although we at times merely waved to each other at a distance from behind the wheels of our respective vehicles (my bookmobile and his school bus), we also began to meet for tea breaks and even lunches. Before long, we had crossed the boundary and were seeing each other outside the library; from there, the relationship really took off.

Here we are three years later, exchanging books as gifts and happy that Gordon's first book is published.[6] I had suspected he might be the man for me when I saw his small apartment was essentially a library with built-in living quarters, and the radio dial was nearly always set on CBC.

Allison's Story

I met my most wonderful husband in the beautiful UCLA Powell Library around 1990. At the time, I was working in the basement of Powell Library and my husband was teaching large undergraduate classes in the atmospheric sciences department. One day, he needed to use the services of my office, so he called to see if he could come over to pick up something. Although it was around 6 p.m., I said, "Sure, come on over, but I have to leave at around six-thirty." I waited for a while and he still had not shown up. So I went to the double wooden front doors of my office and flung the door open. Unknown to me, my future husband had just arrived and was reaching for the doorknob of the door I flung open. He has the bad habit of leaning forward and down into the door where it opens as he is turning the door knob. That habit intersected with my bad habit of opening doors quickly. So the door hit him in the head. I said, "Are you all right?" He had his eyes closed and was somewhat swooning around when he said, hesitantly, "I, uh, I'm OK." I told him I thought he needed to sit down for a while or go to the emergency room. So he sat down and we started talking.

We got married about two years later at the Athenaeum, the beautiful faculty club at the California Institute of Technology. We spent our honeymoon night in the suite where Albert Einstein and his wife lived while at Cal Tech. This just goes to show you can find almost anything you want in life at the library—it is truly the place of great beginnings!

I open doors much more slowly now.

Venessa's Story

As a diligent law student, intent on making up for lack of natural ability with hard work, I spent countless hours in the Drake University Law Library. I carefully selected my study spot by focusing on those locations where I would be left alone, where others would not lure me into idle conversation or entice me away for more social endeavors. One favorite study spot was a small, yet comfortable room in the basement of the Carnegie building. The room's size was, in my view, perfectly designed to deter those who might want to join me without being cramped. My strategy was to further deter other students from inhabiting the room by spreading my books and papers generously across the only two tables. This generally worked until one fellow classmate began sharing the room with me, seemingly clueless as to my desire to claim the room for my exclusive use. I now understand that he was not clueless at all, but determined. After several offers to cook pasta for me, I finally agreed to accompany him to a baseball game . . . all the while not fully appreciating his romantic aspirations. I soon came to appreciate those aspirations and his home-style Italian cooking more.

That was twelve years, four jobs, and two children ago. Now, happily married, I work on the same campus where it all began. A new law library has been built on campus and the Carnegie building is used for administrative offices. I often think that if my office was ever moved to the basement of Carnegie that my life would have come full circle. In any event, it did all begin in the library. Today, he still thinks I'm a study geek and I still think he can be clueless, but at the end of the day this library romance paid off.

Roelof's Story

It was December 29, 1969, and the sixties were almost over. I was enrolled at the Frederick Muller Academy, the Amsterdam library school. The big canteen had to be refurbished, and a group of students met every night to accomplish this job. On the third night, as I painted the wall in violet with big strokes, a nice girl with soft eyes and beautiful long hair (and legs) at my right side did the same, with great zeal. The next day we continued, while from the loudspeakers boomed "Lay, Lady, Lay" by a very tender Bob Dylan and ruby wine went down during the breaks.

It was real love at first sight. We acquired a house, two daughters, and a dog. Everything which my wife, a librarian too, undertook, she did with great zeal. But it was her first and last paint job. When I paint at home, she doesn't stop criticizing me. It has to be perfect!

That night, long ago, at the "Herengracht," that nice Dutch canal, my wife must have been in search of a painter-librarian or the like. But "Lay, Lady, Lay" remains a wonderful song.

Michele's Story

On October 11, 1998, I attended a jazz concert at the Oak Park Library and so did Ken. When the concert was over, he came over to me and started a conversation. This led to us exchanging phone numbers and we began dating. A few months later, we knew we wanted to spend our lives together and we became engaged in May 1999. Our wedding was in May 2000, and, although we were fifty-five and sixty-two (both of us had been married before), we fully expected to have twenty or more years with each other. Unfortunately, Ken was diagnosed in 2003 with a rare kind of cancer (angiosarcoma), and he lost his battle with it on April 5, 2004. The fact is we didn't meet reading or checking out books; we met because this particular library had events such as art displays and concerts.

We Married in 1995—Kathy Husband

Being a librarian and obviously hooked on reading, I began to attend a book discussion group at the Lakewood Library in March of 1991.[7] The book being discussed was *Elmer Gantry*. There I met one of the few male participants, at a time before book groups were coming into their own. He told me his name was Rich Husband. I asked, "Are you either?" and he said "Neither."

Not being a material girl, I went with the "single" cue, and the rest is history. We were married in 1995 and continue to enjoy many a quiet evening together with our noses in a good book. We also continue to frequent the library's various book groups.

Sheila's Story

In 1991 I was hired as the new volunteer services coordinator for the Talking Book Services for the Blind at the Idaho State Library. I was newly divorced and pretty sour on men, having had a rocky time of it. My new job was very exciting. I was to oversee the operation of a small but professional recording studio where volunteers recorded local Idaho books on tape to add to our Talking Book Library collection. The program was pretty small (only eight registered volunteers) and I was the first full-time coordinator. The first thing I did was to get familiar with the equipment by listening to some of the tapes that were in progress. I loaded up one tape by a volunteer named Greg. I had an instant connection with his deep, resonant baritone, and I could hardly wait to meet the person behind it. I checked his volunteer records and saw that he hadn't come in to the library on a regular basis for quite some time.

I couldn't let this voice get away so I started calling him a couple of times a week to assure him that we still wanted him to come in, and that I would be here to work with him. When we finally met, I was thrilled to see that he looked as good as he sounded, maybe even better.

But the best part was that he was a genuinely nice guy! We worked together in the intimate setting of the recording studio for a couple of months. By that time I had decided he was married, since his main topic in conversation was his kids. When he asked me out, I said it was a very tempting offer, but I didn't date married men. He replied that he had been divorced for nine years and he would show me the papers if I needed to see them. We dated for a year and now we are about to celebrate our twelfth wedding anniversary.

Maija's Story

My boyfriend, Howard, and I had been dating for about four years when he proposed. During the time we dated, I graduated and received my MLS, and worked in two libraries. Howard has never worked in a library but loves libraries and books. In August of 2003, he surprised me with a visit while I was working at the library. He gave me a wrapped gift which I set aside in order to assist some patrons. When I was free, I said thank you and was thinking I would take my gift home to open in private. Howard told me to open the gift now. I opened it: it was a book and still I didn't have a clue! The book said "Ever After" and had a picture on the cover. I opened the book and inside was a beautiful engagement ring. At that moment, he knelt down on one knee and asked me to be his wife. I said yes! My coworkers threw me a shower in the library as well! We were married in December of 2003.

Theresa's Story

Curtis and I had been peripheral figures in each other's lives since childhood (same schools, and so on), but had never really gotten to know each other well. When I was hired as a library page at the Civic Center Library in Torrance, California, in the summer of 1988, Curtis, already on staff for two years, was assigned to train me. Just eighteen, I developed a serious crush on him. Although I didn't know it at the time, the feeling was mutual.

His assigned section ended where mine began, and we would spend our shifts shelf-reading the point where the two met. Our daily talks surely led to the cleanest row in library history!

When I started college I quit my job, only to return in the summer of 1989. Curtis was dating a fellow employee, but we quickly renewed our friendship. Each day we would spend our fifteen-minute break together. I pined for him for years, but when he and his girlfriend broke up, I was seeing someone else! Finally, in the winter of 1992 we were both available, and Curtis took the plunge and asked me out. After years of friendship, we quickly fell into the role of boyfriend and girlfriend, and became exclusive in April of 1993. By May, we knew we were in love.

In October of 1993, six months after becoming a couple, I arrived to work and settled in. The public address system crackled to life, and I heard Curtis's voice say, "I have a very important announcement to make." His shift didn't start for another two hours, so I was a bit perplexed, wondering why he was at work early. His next sentence answered my question and changed my life forever. "Theresa Lynn Calhoun, will you make me the happiest man alive by taking my hand in marriage?" Tears formed in my eyes. My coworkers turned to me, eyes wide. I stumbled up the stairs, and met Curtis, stumbling down. "Yes!" I exclaimed, falling into his embrace. He revealed a most stunning diamond ring and slipped it on to my finger. Time stopped. Soon we were surrounded by coworkers. "What did she say, what did she say?" they asked. As we accepted their congratulations, we were informed that patrons were approaching the service desk, anxious for my answer.

I approached the PA system, my voice thick with emotion, and answered, "Yes. I love him so much!" The stillness of the library was broken by applause.

Curtis and I celebrated our tenth wedding anniversary this year. He has moved on to other career fields, but multiple promotions later, I am still with the Torrance Public Library. After a stressful shift on the public service desk, I still pause on the stairwell at the spot where my soul mate and I agreed to spend forever loving each other.

Donna's Story

On a warm May afternoon I had just gotten off work at the Saskatoon Public Library in Saskatoon, Saskatchewan and realized that I needed to take the bus home. Normally I would have my car but I had taken it in for an oil change. I stood and waited very patiently. At that moment I noticed a City of Saskatoon half-ton truck pulling up at the corner of the street. I saw a gorgeous, massively built, dark-haired young man. I smiled at him and he smiled at me. He continued to drive by the library and down the street. A few minutes passed and the Saskatoon city transit bus pulled up. Just as I was about to get onto the bus, this handsome young man came around the corner a second time. Smiling to myself, I climbed onto the bus and sat down. This young hunk pulled up to the bus window and mouthed, "Where do you work?" "The library!" I answered.

At that moment the bus pulled away from the stop and we were separated. I continued to ponder on this man while the bus made a number of other stops. Finally the bus reached the terminal (approximately two to three kilometers from the stop where I climbed in). There, honking the horn, was this dream man. He motioned for me to get off the bus and he would drive me to my destination. The horns behind this city vehicle continued to blare. I continued to shake my head no, I would not get off the bus. In a moment of weakness, looking into those dark eyes, I was transfixed and suddenly I was off the bus and into this stranger's vehicle.

Six months later we were married and have been for more than twenty years.

Prewar Romance in the U.K. National Library—Jill Kempshall

My parents (Rhoda and Jimmy Hines) met during the 1930s in the great Round Reading Room of the British Museum Library in London (later to become the British Library). My father worked there as a cataloger; my mother was assistant to the editor of the *Subject Index to Periodicals* (now the *British Humanities Index*), which was then published by the Library Association. Her work took her regularly to the British Museum Library to consult material held there. At the time access to the more valuable material kept in the library was via a corridor which was entered through a locked door. Readers had to ring a bell and a member of library staff would open the door and check their reader's ticket before allowing them through. After a few visits my mother became aware of a young man who always seemed to be in a great hurry to get to the door to open it for her—of course this was no mere coincidence. My father, who was often on Reading Room duty, had spotted the pretty young girl who stood out amongst the other rather more elderly readers who frequented the library in that era.

Their whispered conversations led to a lifelong romance—with each other and with the library. My mother loved hiking and camping, while my father was a keen cyclist, so he joined her camping group and they bought a tandem on which they covered many miles. After their wedding in 1940 they went off on the faithful tandem for a honeymoon spent in a tent in the West Country—war had started and they were lucky to be together for a while. Their happiness was short-lived as they were soon to be separated for five years while my father was with the British Army in India and Sri Lanka. Meanwhile work on the *Subject Index to Periodicals* was made very difficult due to the air raids on London, while the supply of European periodicals to index had dried up after the fall of France. Some British publications ceased—sometimes because premises had been destroyed, or even due to a shortage of paper. My mother and other members of the editorial team were moved to an office in the National Library of Wales in Aberystwyth and the *Subject Index* continued to be published through the war years.

After the war my father returned to work in the British Library, and as a young child I was occasionally taken to his office which was an Aladdin's cave of new books—a delight to see for a postwar child brought up on secondhand belongings in those years of austerity. When her children were teenagers my mother returned to work, this time employed in the library itself, to work on the British Museum National Library catalog. She and my father traveled to work there daily until their retirement.

I too came under the spell of the British Library when I was employed as a student worker in the Reading Room during two university summer vacations, some thirty years after my parents had first met there. So it has certainly played a major part in our family life!

My mother died in September 2004, aged ninety-two, but my ninety-six-year-old father still has vivid memories of the romance of that particular library.

Notes

1. William J. Clinton, *My Life* (New York: Alfred A. Knopf, 2004), 181–82.

2. Hillary Rodham Clinton, *Living History* (New York: Scribner, 2003), 52.

3. Laura Orr, e-mail to editor, November 24, 2004.

4. Carolynn Prelutsky, e-mail to editor, October 14, 2004.

5. Andrea Lynn, "Love for the Library Revealed in 10 Millionth Volume." *News Bureau*, University of Illinois at Urbana-Champaign, 2003, at www.news.uiuc.edu/news/03/1003tenmillion.html (accessed October 20, 2004).

6. Gordon Phinn, *Eternal Life and How to Enjoy It* (Charlottesville, VA: Hampton Roads Press, 2004).

7. Previously published in 2002 in "50 Stories for 50 Years," a publication of Jefferson County Public Library (Colorado, U.S.A.).

CHAPTER THREE

Reading Room Romance

It was a reading room romance, told to an audience at the ALA/CLA Conference in Toronto in 2002, that sparked my interest in writing this book. In the question period, when I asked the audience if they agreed with me that libraries can inspire the emotions and are very romantic places, many hands shot up. A man offered to tell his story.

I have to refer to him as "a man" because to my regret I have been unable to locate this librarian. While his story has been the impetus for this book, and I have put out many calls to try to find him, I have so far had no response. So he remains "the unknown romantic" of this book.

He told us they met at the university library. Creatures of habit, they would always sit at the same study table. He was too shy to say anything to her. Weeks would go by with little more than a shy smile. One day without really knowing why, they began to exchange a little conversation. Gradually they were talking regularly, taking coffee breaks together, and moving closer at the table.

Their romance blossomed over time, and eventually they married. Hearing that the library was changing its furnishings, they went to the administration and asked if they could buy "their" study table. The administration agreed, and the deal was done. Every day they are reminded of how they met. Their study table is now their dining table in their happy home.

Coach Joe Paterno of Penn State University and his wife Sue met in the reading room of the Pattee Library, when she was tutoring his football players. They clearly have a love of libraries, and fond memories of how the library brought them together, because they have been generous benefactors of Penn State. Thanks to their large donation, the expanded wing of what was formerly known as East Pattee Library has been named the Paterno Library in their honor.[1]

Jane's Story

Jane was a junior in a small program where all the students usually studied in the departmental library reading room. She was quietly besotted with George, a senior.

She had deliberately picked a study space at the opposite corner from where George regularly studied. That way, she could surreptitiously observe him with her books propped open. George had thick, jet black, shiny hair, deep blue eyes, and long black eyelashes. As she sat translating Latin love poetry, she would look over at George and ache with longing.

The highlight of the school year was the end-of-year ball, when the students would wear elegant formal dress, drink champagne, and dance all night. Jane silently begged for George to invite her. As the day of the ball grew closer, the other students in the program were pairing off and making plans, while she sat covertly staring at George, willing him to ask her. He hasn't asked anyone else in the program to go; tomorrow he'll ask me, she told herself as each day passed.

The day of the big event arrived, and still she had no invitation. To add to her distress, George didn't appear in the library that day. The other students were leaving early to make preparations for the evening. Jane was utterly miserable. She reached a point that anyone who has experienced unrequited love will recognize, where the only thing that could make her feel better was to make herself suffer even more. She decided to grab a sandwich from the cafeteria and return to the reading room for a solitary evening of study.

The evening wore on. Jane was alone in the reading room. She dimmed the lights so that half of the room was in semi-darkness. She switched on a brass reading lamp and decided to make her misery complete by putting aside love poetry for some Roman military history. Suddenly, she heard the familiar squeak of the reading room door opening. As she looked up apprehensively, the subject of her dreams appeared through the gloom in front of her. Speechless, she stared at him. "I thought everyone would have been at the ball," he said.

She blurted something out about being behind on her Cicero translation. Cicero was his favorite author, he responded. They spent a companionable couple of hours (during which time she doesn't recall breathing at all) side by side, while he patiently explained the intricacies of military formations and Ciceronian syntax.

When her heart was so full she felt transported to a higher existence, George suggested they go to a nearby pub for a beer. As she sat in the crammed and smoky bar, sipping her beer and laughing at his jokes while she gazed up into those blue eyes, she thought that Cinderella could not have been happier than she was that evening. She didn't have the carriage, the gown, or the glass slippers, but she *did* have the company of a classically handsome Prince Charming for a couple of hours.

The following year when she received a Valentine's card that said "Guess who?" she was delirious, because she knew (or so she thought) his handwriting so well. She was a little hurt that he had addressed the envelope to "Miss J. Hulk" (her surname was Huck). She generously put it down to his sense of humor, rather than a comment on her proportions. It wasn't until she was graduating that she discovered by chance that the card had been sent by his roommate, who mistakenly thought that was her name.

George and Jane never dated. They became casual friends after the evening of the ball—casual at least on George's side, unrequited anticipation on hers. He left the university to become a teacher at an exclusive school, where he still teaches over thirty years later. George never married, but Jane did.

Nancy's Story

My husband and I met in the reserve book room at Oregon State University's Kerr Library in Corvallis, Oregon, on October 14, 1971. I was a sophomore and David was just returning to school after two years in the army, including a year in Vietnam. I always studied at the library so Dave saw me regularly, and one day he finally got up the nerve to talk to me. I was studying for an organic chemistry test and it wasn't going well, so I was not in a particularly friendly mood. But by the end of the evening I had agreed to see a movie with him the following weekend.

Our courtship took place largely in the library. Dave was a civil engineering major and I was in microbiology, so we both needed a lot of study time. We both spent many an hour in the library, often distracted from studying by writing notes to each other in our textbooks. I've saved my organic chemistry book all these years because it has the most love notes written in it! It was at the library where Dave asked me to "go steady," the term we used back then meaning an exclusive relationship. Love continued to grow and we were engaged in the summer of 1972 and married in August of 1973. Last year we celebrated thirty years of marriage.

In an interesting footnote, our oldest daughter, Cheryl, is currently studying to get her master's in library and information science at the University of British Columbia. Libraries must be in our genes!

Andrew's Story

I was a third-year undergraduate student at Carleton University in Ottawa, Ontario. There was a table in the main library that was a little tucked out of the way—near some little-used reference material and atlases. One day I was doing some reading when I saw the woman of my dreams, with a brown bob and green eyes. I fell in love instantly, but being shy I was not sure how to approach her. I asked her for the time, she told me rather curtly, and I fled. I went home and called my best friend, who scolded me about not approaching her. "You'll never see her again, man," I recall him saying.

I decided to test the odds of that by returning to the table, hoping my dream lady was a creature of habit. Happily she was, and a few days later there we were once more. Again seeking a conversational gambit, I asked if I could look at her map. She sort of said yes, but mostly waved toward the stacks of atlases, explaining that the map she was looking at was fairly specialized—a linguistic map of North American native peoples.

Despite the partial brush-off, I persisted in chatting a bit, and eventually gathered the courage to ask her for coffee. Being a sensible person, she declined, but agreed to study together again and then see from there.

She was inclined to take it slowly, but two weeks later she was in love with me too, and six months later we were living together. We've been together ever since (more than ten years) and have been happily married for seven of those years. I have since found out that my wife Brenda and her roommates all preferred that table, fondly calling it the "secret table." We made it a table of fate, and there's no secret about that! Thanks to the Carleton University Library for bringing us together in such a wholesome fashion!

Corban's Story

My wife and I first laid eyes on each other in the library our first year at college. I was studying for a biology test when I looked over my shoulder to another table and saw a girl sitting there studying. I thought to myself that she was very attractive. As I was studying I had the unfortunate habit of leaning back in my seat. One second I was balanced on two legs of my chair and the next second I was falling head over heels backward. This is where my lovely bride comes into the story. She was the only person nearby at the time of the event and the only person to see my blunder. She began to laugh and laugh, and laugh, and laugh. Every time I had the nerve to look her direction we would make eye contact and she would start giggling. This continued to go on until I decided to go to my dorm room. As I was leaving I passed her study table and told her that I would stop distracting her from her studies. I was out the door of the library, when my bride-to-be chased me down and introduced herself to me. Evidently she felt bad for all the giggling and wanted to apologize for adding to my already embarrassing moment.

The story was just beginning there. When I returned to my room, I couldn't settle down to my studies and decided I would head back to the library to check my e-mail, knowing full well that the server was down. As I was walking back into the library I was met once again by my beauty. To my "shock," she informed me that the computers were not working and so I politely walked my new friend back to her dormitory and we struck up a conversation that led to friendship, which led to romance.

About a year or so later my beautiful friend and I were sitting at a table together studying for our respective classes. I don't know what possessed me to verbalize my feeling right there in the middle of a busy library but I blurted out the words, "I love you." I just sat there with my heart pounding in my chest, stunned by what I just said, and I believe that she was stunned also. She had been reading but after I had spilled the beans she was just sitting there looking at pages. We didn't make very much eye contact after that but just sat in our seats, hearts thumping. It did take about three months for her to verbalize the same affection, but this happened just outside the library. Another first for me happened across the street from the library. We had our first kiss! It was just a peck but it took both of us a seeming eternity to build up the nerve to peck away.

We hold fond memories of our relationship in the library. I even used a reference to our first meeting in my proposal. I told her that from the very first time I laid my eyes on her I had "fallen" for her and that I wanted to fall for her for the rest of my life.

I Lost My Innocence in
a Library—John Tate

It was the fall of 1969 and I was a first-year student at the University of Winnipeg. The sexual revolution might have already started, but if so, I was definitely not one of its casualties. The new wave of permissiveness changing the mores of society had left me and my circle of friends stranded on the beach of celibacy.

There was, however, a girl in my English class. She was, as a well-known advertisement notes, a goddess. One day she sat beside me and asked me a question about an assignment—I was paralyzed for the rest of the lecture. A day or two later she noticed me when she came into class and smiled right at me. She sat somewhere else but from that point I was helplessly, hopelessly, in love.

I began to fantasize. I imagined the two of us on a beach, watching a sunset, or in a meadow, leaning against a tree reading poems by John Keats. A professor had read "Ode on a Grecian Urn" to our class, making it so sensuous, in an antiseptic way, that I could conceive nothing more romantic. She was purity, the epitome of spiritual love, so only in my darkest thoughts could I envision the ultimate reward, a stolen kiss, taken on her doorstep when we said goodnight.

I was working on an essay in the library when she came in and sat at a table by the window, the light from behind haloing her head. I don't need to catalog the physical sensations that overwhelmed me; if you've ever been in love you know them. A minute later, a scruffy-looking guy sat across from her and they began to whisper. My heart stopped. No, it was impossible; a deity would never sully herself with a specimen so detestable.

She wrote a note, folded it, and passed it to him. He unfolded it, read it, and smiled. Then they got up and left. The note was still sitting on the table. I picked it up, opened it. "Take me home," it started. What she wanted to do at home was explicit, the Anglo-Saxon expletive jumping off the page and settling in my bowel. I haven't been able to look at another Keats poem since.

Catherine's Story

It happened in the library at Waterloo Lutheran University with the first hint of spring, in the year 1965. I dropped my armload of heavy reference books at the end of a long table and sat there to study, instead of at the usual cloistered desk. I couldn't help noticing a good-looking guy with bright blond hair, who had come to sit at the other end of the table. He was nonchalantly fidgeting with everything, concentrating on nothing, with an apparent air of lightheartedness about him. My main impression was that he was likely a freshman about to flunk out.

It was near exams, so I was back in the library a couple of days later. This time, I decided to return to the same table, instead of picking a study spot haphazardly. Maybe the blond would be back! And he was . . . rapping his pencil, gazing everywhere except at his books. The next day again we were together at the same table, only this time, as I left the library he joined me with an invitation for coffee at the university's Torque Room. It was delightful and the beginning of my caffeine addiction. I remember how he "wowed" me with his mastery of the game of Xs and Os during that first meeting, his huge smile, and his jovial laugh.

Our first real date was the next night at a dance in a church basement. There was almost no one there, but we didn't need anyone else that night, as we danced and laughed. Really, he was a show in himself.

It was at a study table in the library that our separate paths converged. We got married and were blessed with three daughters and twenty-five years of laughter. As it turned out, Mike wasn't a failing freshman at all, but would soon become a teacher, inspiring high school students with his laughter and great love of knowledge.

Beryl's Story

I fell in love with libraries as an undergraduate slumped over tomes of Shakespeare criticism on cold winter afternoons in the Reading Room of Newcastle University with the metallic green-shaded lamps throwing pools of light over the desks. I fell in love with another William at Sheffield University because he wore a beautiful blue shirt and had brown eyes and floppy dark hair. We had many assignations in the library stacks by the bound volumes of Punch until he swept me off my feet by inviting me to help him to choose an Anglepoise lamp from a shop in Broomhill. Over thirty years later the shop is still there and the Anglepoise is still casting its light over the heaps of bills on our desk.

Raphaelle's Story

After two years of searching aimlessly and forlornly for a boyfriend in the bars of Manhattan, just when I had given up on love altogether, this guy sat down next to me in the Avery Library at Columbia. I had gone to Avery to study for a biology midterm for the entire weekend because I was nearly failing the class. We sat next to each other for a few hours, both totally absorbed in our studying. Finally, I asked him if he had any gum. He didn't, but we started chatting. He walked me home, asked me out, and moved to California with me. After five years together, he just asked me to marry him. If Avery weren't such a preppy name, I would probably name our kid Avery, if we have kids. We've had a lovely romance.

May's Story

In 1967 I went to the Baptist College in Manchester, England to continue research for a master's degree in politics. The first day I sat down to study, the Senior Student went by and said he had to tell me the rules of the college. We got engaged two days later and married at the end of the year. In his address at our wedding the principal of the college referred to marriages being made in heaven, which meant the college could be regarded as an outpost!

My husband, Tony, became the executive director of the Leprosy Mission for England and Wales and was an advisor to Diana, Princess of Wales. Sadly, he died of heart trouble a year ago. We had been married thirty-six years and have one fabulous daughter.

I did finish my master's!

Bridget's Story

I met my husband on the ninth floor of the Hesburgh Library at the University of Notre Dame. We were both beginning grad school. We watched each other for a few days as we entered and exited our windowless study carrels to take frequent breaks. My husband (to be) asked me to watch his laptop while he went to get a cup of coffee. This started our conversation. For me it was really love at first sight. It took my husband a little longer to figure it all out.

We continue to be very fond of libraries and support this precious public good in the communities where we live. Especially in the early years of our marriage we would visit the wonderful libraries in our Indianapolis and Columbus, Ohio, communities, for our cheap date nights out, sipping coffee, enjoying the magazines, checking sections we would otherwise not visit, and enjoying community programming.

My husband now serves on the board of our local library here in the Detroit area.

Note

1. Daryl Lang, "Paternos Dedicate Renovated Wing of Library," *The Digital Collegian*, 2000, at www.collegian.psu.edu/archive/2000/09/09–11–00tdc/09–11–00 dnews-5.asp (accessed October 21, 2004).

CHAPTER FOUR

The Romance of Reference

Working at the reference desk, by its very nature, involves meeting many people every day. In an academic library, reference librarians meet not only student patrons but also other academic staff of the university. The resourcefulness of reference librarians has impressed many. Thus, there can be ample opportunity for a potential romance.

Michael's Story

My boyfriend and I met at the reference desk at the Miller Nichols Library at the University of Missouri–Kansas City. I am a reference librarian and he is the professor of costume design for the theater department. He is completely lost in a library and during the summer session he had no student assistants to assign his research to. He had to come to the reference desk to ask for help in tracking down pictures of clothing from the 1930s so he could start designing the costumes for *The Front Page*. He had been trying for a while on his own with no luck. He finally came to the desk to ask for help and within minutes I had several back issues of *Life* and *Harpers Bazaar* for him to look through. Since we do not have a color copier in the library, I let him check out a couple volumes of the magazines so he could get them copied elsewhere. He was so happy with the service I was able to give him that he asked me out to dinner the next week. (It did not hurt that he thought I was cute too.) This happened in August 2003, and we have been together ever since.

Lynn's Story

My husband and I met at the library of the American Museum of Natural History in New York City. I was a reference librarian, he a graduate student in animal behavior. I gave an orientation session to a number of graduate students and he was among them. I noticed him much later hanging around the library a lot. We started talking one day and he told me much later that I was the most helpful librarian he had encountered and that he learned a lot at my session. We ended up going out. He introduced me to the two snakes that were in his lab, two eleven-foot-long large snakes, one a boa and one a python. Good thing I liked animals!

That was back in 1982, and we were married in 1986. I am still a librarian; he is an entomologist and works in neuroscience here at the University of Illinois. When we moved from Boston to Illinois in 1995 with our two kids, one five weeks old, we also had a python in the U-Haul. Betty grew to be almost twelve feet and now lives with someone in Indiana—she was *too* big.

John's Story

I met Maureen, my wife of more than twenty-six years, in the library. As a young reference librarian in my first professional position at a medical school library that also served a school of nursing, my future wife, a third-year nursing student at that time, asked a reference question regarding postpartum depression (she maintains it was on teenage mothers' prenatal care). Even though I was dating someone regularly at the time, I knew within thirty seconds that I would marry her. I had seen her only once before in the library with a man who had been her former boyfriend (I later found out), but I hadn't thought anything special about her at the time.

I asked her after a minute or two of negotiating the question to come into my office so we could chat. I asked her a bunch of questions, including asking for her phone number. I called her about five days later for a date, and she was anxiously waiting to hear from me. We went out later that week in mid-January. Within two weeks we were engaged and we were married by Thanksgiving weekend of that year.

We subsequently moved to another state and while I was working at another medical school library, Maureen worked at the university hospital on the overnight shift. I developed a friendship with a single reference librarian with whom I shared daily lunches. One day she had a third-year medical student ask her a question and I saw the exact same look in her eyes as I had seen in my wife's when we met. I told her later that she would be marrying the man and she laughed, although she thought he was handsome. Seven months later they were wed and remain happily married after twenty-three years.

Yvonne's Story

In 1974, I was a reference librarian working the evening shift in my hometown library. A coworker had given my name to her neighbor, whom she said was tall and single. He came to meet me that evening after closing and took me out for a drink. For three more years we met after work, shared calls surreptitiously at the reference desk, and finally were married in 1978.

One day while on the reference desk, I was buzzed by our receptionist saying that "Tom" was on the phone for me. He often called me at the library and I was about to pick up the receiver and greet him with a tender "hi, sweetie." Fortunately, my guardian angel must have inspired me with a touch of caution, so I merely said a business-like hello. It's a good thing, because it was my boss, also a Tom. What a close call. It wouldn't have been too cool to address him as "sweetie"!

For twenty-six more happy years, we attended library conferences together and he met and enjoyed all my library colleagues. He was quite popular as a dance partner at conference parties, and I was glad to share him for a little while. Sadly, he passed away in the spring of 2004, but he gave a great life to the librarian he had once "checked out" on a rainy summer night.

Steve's Story

Years ago, most database searches were done through intermediaries; that is, a patron needing a search would make an appointment for a librarian trained in BRS or Dialog command language to do the search for him or her. I was one such librarian, and in 1991 my boss handed me a form filled out by one such patron. Standard procedure was to call the patron and arrange an interview, perhaps doing the search in the patron's presence to permit immediate feedback.

Oddly enough, this patron's phone number included an exchange used in Urbana, Illinois—where I'd lived before moving to my current job. So when I called her, after conducting a reference interview and setting a time and date for our online search, I took the liberty of asking her if she lived in Urbana. No, it turned out to be a coincidence. But she impressed me during the conversation as a very intelligent and vibrant woman.

I still remember the date we set for the search—May 28, 1991. I also still remember what she wore—pink blouse, purple skirt, and matching purple pumps—but what really caught my attention was her dazzling smile. Somehow, it made me feel, well, important.

We spent two hours using the ERIC database to research her topic. We also made some small talk, and to my surprise I found myself telling her things I don't usually tell people I've just met. She delighted me with her intelligence and positive approach to any difficulties we encountered. (Her beauty didn't hurt matters either.)

At the end of the two hours, I knew I wanted a date with her more than I'd ever wanted anything in my life. But I hesitated. After all, we had a professional relationship; technically, she was my client. Besides, a woman has a right to expect that her librarian won't hit on her! Still, I really wanted to get to know her better. I finally decided to throw professionalism to the wind and fabricated a flimsy excuse to see her again: "Perhaps we can further discuss your research over lunch?" Subsequent conversations have confirmed my suspicion at the time that she saw right through my ploy. But she said yes anyway.

We were married seventeen months later.

Tim's Story

When I was in library school, I worked in the reference library at my university. I remember there was a very cute girl who used to come into the library and use the computers near the information desk where I worked. I always admired her when she walked past, but she never looked up or made eye contact, so I couldn't even smile at her. It looked to be another case of an anonymous unrequited crush from afar. About a year later, I met a very charming graduate student on an online dating service. We hit it off immediately, and sent each other huge, epic e-mails every day for several weeks. Although we both attended the same university, we were unable to meet because she was doing dissertation research in another city. After about ten days, we had our first phone date, and after that we talked on the phone every day in addition to our e-mail correspondence.

We traded pictures over e-mail, and, although I thought she was very cute, none of her pictures seemed to look the same. One picture in particular seemed very familiar to me, but I couldn't put my finger on it. Then one night, as I was lying in bed after a long telephone conversation, it occurred to me: she's the cute girl from the library! When I called her the next day, I asked her if she used to use the computers near the information desk during the semester in question. She said yes.

A few weeks later, we finally met in person, and I was able to confirm with absolute certainty that my online romance was one and the same with the anonymous unrequited crush from a year earlier.

We're getting married in 2005.

Lynda's Story

When I was in the second year of my MLS studies, I worked part time at two local university libraries. Both positions were on the reference desk and designed to give me that important hands-on experience that potential graduates need, as well as much-needed extra cash. One of the universities was known more for its football team's reputation than its academics. So a typical shift on the evening reference desk involved answering some pretty dumb questions. For example, one young man actually asked if there were any books on science.

One Tuesday evening in early January, a different sort of student came up to the desk. Definitely not a first-year student, he was tanned and very outdoorsy looking, although not a jock. Aha, a skier, I thought. He was searching for information on South Africa and apartheid (this was the early eighties). He was a graduate student studying political science. I think I spent the last twenty minutes of my shift talking to him over a pile of social science abstracts.

The following Tuesday night he came in again and discovered that I also worked on Thursday evenings. On Thursday night, he came in yet again and asked to meet me for coffee after my shift; thus began a familiar pattern. We began dating and did so for several years. I graduated and went out into the real world to pursue my career and he remained a perpetual graduate student.

In the end, he never did finish his degree and we eventually broke up. But I'll always have the tale of how I was picked up while working at the reference desk.

Nada's Story

I met my husband at the library's reference department. He was a regular patron who checked the newspapers and investment newsletters. I must have known him for some ten years before he decided to ask me out—neither of us was ready to enter the relationship until then.

We also frequented the same church. According to my husband, that was the determining factor. In April, we will have been married for three years. He took an early retirement five years ago while I continue to work. We look forward to the day when both of us will be retired, but I do enjoy my work as a local history librarian and archivist.

Linda's Story

I didn't expect to find love at the reference desk, but after I'd helped a graduate student in the school psychology program with his interlibrary loan requests, he started hanging around just to talk. Jeff[1] was a reentry student, divorced and in his early forties, who had decided he really wanted to work with kids. He was a gentle giant, and his beard reminded me of one of the professors I'd had a crush on in library school.

We chatted over the weeks during the fall term and found we had similar attitudes and tastes in many things. It was actually the red licorice that was the clincher. One day he showed up with a bag and said he just thought I'd like it. How could he have known my lifelong addiction?

By Thanksgiving we were an item. In January he gave me a promise ring for my birthday, and we started window shopping for the real thing. I started looking at babies in a different light, wondering if we'd have tow-headed little ones together.

Unfortunately I got a new job that was a ten-hour drive from where he was offered a position and we weren't able to sustain the long-distance relationship. Sometimes I regret that I didn't let him give up his first job in his new career and just move in with me. Maybe I should have tried just a little harder and we would have made it. I've lost track of Jeff and sometimes I wonder if he is still in the state and working with troubled kids as he had planned. I guess I'll never know.

Note

1. Pseudonym.

CHAPTER FIVE

Student Assistants and Romance

The Edmonton Journal tells a story of a lasting love that was kindled against the odds within a library:[1]

Golden Couple Celebrate Love, Survival in "Sea of Whites"—Elizabeth Ferguson

Ardis and Krishan Kamra of Edmonton are celebrating their golden wedding anniversary. They're also celebrating the survival of their interracial relationship, despite strong opposition in the 1950s. Ardis was the granddaughter of the late Charles Stewart, Alberta's last Liberal premier, and came from a Caucasian Anglican household in Camrose. Krishan, a Sikh, left his home province of Punjab, India, in 1948, as a result of the tumultuous partition of India and Pakistan the year before.

At 19, Krishan traveled alone to Canada, student visa in hand. He first studied at the University of Saskatchewan, and then transferred to the University of Alberta. Krishan said that although his skin color and ethnic background were different, he felt welcomed by Canadians. At times he even received more favorable treatment as a "brown man."

"I really never thought that I was different except when I looked in the mirror," he said. "But in a sea of whites, I stood out."

Ardis and Krishan met amongst the bookshelves of the U of A's first library in May 1951. Ardis, a student library assistant, was overseeing the arrival of books at a new building that would open as the Rutherford Library the following year. Krishan was a student hired by the U of A's building department to haul the crates of books. He was smitten by Ardis's "beautiful smile."

"I couldn't bring the crates of books back to her fast enough," Krishan said, chuckling. "I'm sure I was the hardest working bookman."

Ardis had seen Krishan around and was equally intrigued. But a "very pretty blonde" library assistant was already vying for his attention.

"She was flirting too much with Krishan," Ardis said with a girlish giggle. "So I decided I would charm him a little."

Krishan was so smitten with Ardis that he couldn't resist making a proposition.

"I just had to say, 'I've got to meet you afterwards,'" he said. Krishan treated Ardis to cantaloupe with ice cream at the university tuck shop that evening. It was the beginning of a beautiful relationship between two students from different worlds. Ardis and Krishan didn't think their mixed relationship was a big deal. But as they became serious, university officials tried to douse the flames of their courtship. In the spring of 1952, Ardis and Krishan held hands during a romantic evening walk in Windsor Park. The U of A's dean of women was waiting for Ardis when she got back.

"She invited me to come in and have a cup of tea with her, and she said that a woman had phoned and complained that she had seen a brown man and a white girl walking hand in hand," Ardis said. "She said, 'You know, the university is responsible for you, Ardis, and you should cool it.'"

But Ardis wasn't fazed by the reprimand. She was in love with Krishan and had no intention of cooling it, even though the dean was a friend of Ardis's family.

"I said I would think about it because it was all I could think of that was polite," Ardis said. "I had a lot of respect for her, but I didn't feel I had to do anything in my personal life that she told me to."

The U of A's dean of men was also opposed. "(He) said our children would have a lot of trouble, that they would be discriminated against, especially in school," Ardis said.

Krishan faced similar criticism. He said the university provost told him he had "no business holding hands with a white girl." Krishan got angry and told the provost he wasn't the chief of police and that it wasn't an academic matter. Krishan said the provost was taken aback and replied, "Get off your high horse."

Friends and family weren't much better. Ardis's parents asked a primate of the Anglican Church, who was also a family friend, to speak with Krishan's family when he traveled to India to attend a conference. The family, who unbeknownst to Krishan had already chosen an Indian bride for him, "strongly hoped the archbishop would be able to break us up," he said. But those who condemned the relationship spoke out in vain. On May 8, 1954, Ardis and Krishan were married at Saint Stephen's College Chapel, a United Church on the U of A campus. Ardis's parents were among the fifteen guests, but they offered no financial support for the event. Her father said he'd give the marriage less than three years. The interracial controversy settled down after the wedding. And despite their initial disapproval, Krishan's family warmed to Ardis during the couple's frequent visits to India.

"My Indian family is wonderful," Ardis said. "It was hard to believe that Canada existed when I was in India. I always wore a sari and I felt like a butterfly." Ardis and Krishan both went on to get doctoral degrees from the University of Washington. Krishan was director of instruction at NAIT from 1962, while Ardis worked almost twenty years in the curriculum development branch of Alberta Education.

The couple had two children, David and Kerri. Kerri says she and her brother grew up in an environment of tolerance. "There are no restrictions on who or what kind of person I could become involved with, in the sense of religion, race, ethnicity," Kerri said.

"'We don't want that kind of person in our family'—that would never happen here. There are no barriers." Kerri's partner is Jewish, and David's partner is from the Dominican Republic. Krishan, who became a Canadian citizen, believes he was one of the earliest immigrants from India to settle in Edmonton. He still marvels at how controversial his relationship with Ardis was in the 1950s.

But despite the heartache they caused their parents, the Kamras know they made the right decision. "I always felt like I was doing the right thing and I still think I'm doing the right thing," Ardis said. "After fifty years, if I had the chance, I would ask her to marry me again," Krishan said.

Dorothy's Story

In September 1995 I transferred to the C. W. Post Campus of Long Island University as an undergraduate student, and before classes started, I applied to the library for a job (taking the suggestion of my academic advisor). I began working in the circulation department. One month later I caught the eye of a handsome young man who worked as a graduate assistant in the Academic Computing Center of the library. The next day we met, and it was love at first sight. Arda had come to the United States one year earlier from Turkey to get his MBA. We began dating, and then in 1996, I left the circulation department and also started working in the Academic Computing Center. Our romance became known to almost everyone in the library—we studied there, worked there, we spent many hours there! We were both going to graduate in May 1997, and we both wanted to get full-time jobs so we could think about getting married.

At the same time, two jobs in different departments of the library (separate budgets, separate department heads) opened up. Arda applied for a job as the operations manager of the cataloging department (backing up their computer system), and I applied for a library assistant job in the acquisitions department. We were both hired, and we started *on the same day*—a totally random day—not the beginning of the month or anything particular—April 13, 1997! Furthermore, the departments were physically located next to each other in the library, and there was an open door in between the two. Out of fifteen to twenty people working in the departments, Arda and I had desks on either side of the door—so we could see each other. We sometimes secretly threw paperclips at each other.

We got married in February 1998, and many people from the library attended the wedding. At our fancy rehearsal dinner, my brother from Los Angeles surprised us with a song he wrote for us called "Library Love." He had secretly e-mailed my sister to find out specific details of our story, and he sang the song to us as he played the guitar the night before our wedding.

We no longer work in the library although we still work for the university. We have now been married for almost seven years, and we have a five-month-old baby boy.

Library Love
(Written by Brian Craig)[2]

> She was young, only twenty-one,
> Wonderin' when she'd find her one true love.
> He burst in to her life with a grin,
> He resolved that it was her heart that he'd win
>
> CHORUS:
>
> They had such different lives, but in each other's eyes
> They found a simple something that nothing could disguise.
> Oh it was library love, felt from the start,
> When she said "Where are you from?" and he captured her heart.
>
> Though the trials would come, true love would not fail
> In this library love, a storybook tale
> She found a friend who was warm and sensitive
> He found eternal hope and a godly way to live
> Sometimes all day long he'd watch her as their love grew strong
> He never gave up hope that to him she would belong.

Kimmetha's Story

I began working as a student assistant at West Georgia College Library in 1983. I worked the circulation desk in the afternoons and shelved in the mornings. Every morning this tall, blond, handsome, bearded, and buff fellow came up to the fourth floor and got off the elevator to study his Latin. Every morning I would do my best to maneuver myself right in front of his table. For six months he never looked up (that I could tell) and never spoke.

My mother had been the director's executive assistant since I had been in the sixth grade. One day in her office—which was all glass and overlooked the current periodical seating section—I saw the guy looking at a magazine. I told my mom, "I am going to get that guy to speak to me."

About a month later (January), he got off the elevator as usual and walked over to his table. I noticed with disappointment he no longer had a beard (darn!) but decided this was the opportunity I had been waiting for. I walked over to his table and used my great pickup line: "Didn't you have a beard last week?" He replied that he did and we began a good thirty- to thirty-five-minute discussion. What a bad student assistant I was—I didn't finish shelving my cart of books that day.

I saw him a week later and he walked right by the circulation desk. He saw me but kept walking. I said, "Tom, aren't you going to speak to me?" He is rather shy and was afraid it was some fluke that I spoke to him the week before. From that point on we dated for four years, got engaged, and now have two wonderful children and a very happy marriage of sixteen years in October 2004. My favorite song is Jimmy Buffett's "Love in the Library."

Cheryl's Story

In my freshman year at the University of Illinois at Urbana-Champaign I got my first library job in the English library. James also got his first job on campus at a library when he was a freshman, but at the art and architecture library two years before me.

Time went by and soon I was looking for extra work. At the end of my sophomore year I started doing work at the main book stacks. A few months before, James had taken a job at the main stacks as well. And so perhaps it was fate, or just good timing, but in May of 2000 James and I ran into each other in the main stacks. We began to talk and laugh and, as I would later admit to him, I began trying to move my schedule around so that I could run into him more frequently.

After a few days he asked for my phone number, which I happily gave him. I only worked in the main stacks for a short time, but in that short time I met the greatest love of my life. Our first date was to the art theater in town where we saw Hitchcock's *Rear Window*, and by the end of the summer we were deeply in love. That fall I studied abroad in Athens, Greece, and James wrote to me every day I was gone, and flew out to meet me in December.

Throughout the next few years we both worked in libraries, and eventually James entered the Graduate School of Library and Information Science at the University of Illinois at Urbana-Champaign where he continued to work in a library.

I have very fond memories of events that took place in the libraries we worked at, like the time James sent a dozen roses to the classics library for my birthday while I was working. And there was the time I locked my keys in my car while it was running, and I had to run to his library to get his key.

Time went by, and two years after beginning library school, James got a job in a library in Maryland, at the same time I was starting library school in Urbana-Champaign. In October of 2003 while visiting James out East he proposed to me, and I of course accepted. Soon we will be married, two librarians who love each other deeply, and understand each other immensely, who met and fell in love in the main stacks at the University of Illinois.

Romance in the Library— George and Nancy Stewart

I still remember the day she came into the Central Park Branch Library, although forty-three years (and forty years of marriage) have since passed. She had an umbrella, an armload of books, and enough personality for several people.

I was sixteen years old and working as a page in our neighborhood branch of the Birmingham Public Library. Nancy and I had attended the same elementary school, but she was a year younger—and you did not speak to kids in the classes below you. We attended the same church, and lived only a few blocks apart. I had seen her around, but that was all.

Nancy was, and is, full of life and loves to talk. On that day she and a girlfriend were just having too much fun in the library. Being in charge (meaning that I was the only one who happened to be at the desk), I went over and told her that she would have to be quiet—or leave. She chose to leave.

A few days later she returned, and her afternoon visits became regular. In little time her smile and "I am not afraid of you" attitude won me over. Instead of asking her to leave, I asked her to share my afternoon break at the soda fountain across the street. I do not remember (and probably did not know at the time) when "like" became "love." But it happened.

When I asked her to leave, there certainly were no thoughts of dating her—much less marrying her. I also had no plans to spend my life at the Birmingham Public Library (BPL). I was simply working at a part-time job so that I could finish high school and attend college. Like many librarians that I have met over the years, I stumbled into a career that I had never considered—and loved it.

By the end of my freshmen year of college we planned to marry. At the end of my sophomore year we married, to the admonitions of many who warned that I would never finish school. If we had known how long the road would be, we might have agreed with them.

From the beginning we knew that both of us could not attend college. I worked part time at the library and Nancy worked full time with the telephone company. Instead of our marriage preventing me from finishing college, Nancy made it possible. But we still had a way to go on this road.

Planning to teach history, I finished my undergraduate work and stayed on at school for my master's. We still remember the day I came home to our little apartment and said, "Honey, we have to have $900 in September for graduate school." You might as well have been talking about the national debt. We lived from paycheck to paycheck, putting our money into little envelopes so that we would not spend it on anything frivolous. She assured me that we would find the necessary funds—and we did.

In graduate school my career plans underwent a major shift. Looking back, it is hard to believe that one's entire life could be changed by such a seemingly unimportant event. While working on a graduate paper (so that I could finish school and get a job teaching) I was in BPL's spectacular Southern history and literature collection. On that day BPL director Fant Thornley strolled through the department. Naturally, I got up and spoke to him. He asked how school was progressing, and what my career plans were. I told him that I hoped to finish graduate school by the following June, and find a teaching job soon after. Mr. Thornley observed that those were fine plans. In the meantime, there was a job open in the Southern collection. Would I be interested in working there until I found a teaching job?

The deed was done. Intentionally or not, Mr. Thornley had trapped me. After working in the Southern collection for a very short time I knew this was where I wanted to spend my working career. But we still had only a limited knowledge of where that career would lead. We were reaching the point when I would be out of school; I would be settled in a career; we could start a family. We did start a family and our first son was born just before Mr. Thornley struck again: if I intended to make librarianship my career, there was no substitute for an MLS degree. The University of Alabama had not yet established its school of library and information science, so my library education would have to be out of state. For three summers I commuted to Emory University in Atlanta. Mr. Thornley held my job and arranged for financial assistance. Nancy kept our home together and watched over our family of two sons.

When I finally finished, coworkers gave Nancy a Ph.T. degree (for Putting Hubby Through). I went on to spend thirty-seven years in BPL's central building, including seventeen years as director. We built a new central library, opened new branches, attempted to close branches, and worked through the inevitable budget cycles of public operations. During all of this Nancy was a coworker. She remained a staunch supporter and an honest critic.

After retiring from BPL, I went to work for a nonprofit consulting organization—Library Service Group. Today, Nancy and I both work for the organization. Our lives have been blessed. It is hard to imagine what my life might have been like if that noisy little gal had not come into the Central Park Branch so long ago.

Stewart's Story

I met my wife in an academic library—we were both graduate trainee librarians in 1983. We first kissed at the end-of-year/Christmas library party. By the following Valentine's Day we were engaged and living together and we married in September 2004. By then we'd gotten places at different library schools, so we lived between them and both commuted. The next Valentine's Day I won a local newspaper competition with a Valentine's verse, which went, if I recall correctly:

> To my luscious librarian
> Keep me on permanent loan
> Don't ever shelve me

We are still married (with two teenage kids), although neither of us is working in libraries—but I'm still working in the very same building where we first met over twenty years ago.

Debbie's Story

In the fall of 1997, I was in my second year of library school and was working part time on Thursday evenings at a local technical college library. One night, while I was at the reference desk, a young man entered the library with a bewildered look on his face. Being the intrepid librarian-in-training that I was, I offered proactive reference service by stating to him that he "looked perplexed" and I offered my assistance. "Perplexed . . . that's a big word," was his reply, and I made some comment as to the fact that since we were in a library, we could look it up in the dictionary.

I proceeded to assist him in locating some information about semiconductors or another type of electrical component. Whatever it was, it doesn't matter, as at the time I was already severely smitten and was having trouble remembering how to compose a sentence.

He continued to visit on Thursday evenings, and always made a point of stopping by to say hi and flirt just a bit. I managed to do a fair amount of flirting myself, even though I had a live-in boyfriend at home. I was very conscious of how nervous I was around him, and worried about whether or not he could tell—I was sure he could, as I was flushed and constantly stammering. Nevertheless, when I drove home in my little Volkswagen on Thursday evenings, I was always in a terrific mood!

I described him to some of the other library staff to see if he was spreading his love around on Monday and Wednesday evenings as well, but no one had seen him. Could he be showing up on Thursdays just to see me?

This went on for about six weeks, until one night when he announced to me that he was finished with his course and was leaving the city to continue running his business in a small mountain town where, remarkably, a local library conference is held every spring. Seizing the opportunity, I told him that I and a group of newly minted librarians would be attending the conference; he offered his tourist rooms as accommodations and his phone number, and I told him I'd see him in the spring. He left, both of us a little sad, and my Thursday nights returned to normal.

Spring came along, exams were completed, and the live-in boyfriend was living elsewhere. I steeled myself to call my library love interest. I was relieved to learn that he remembered who I was and was happy to hear from me! My graduating group made plans for the conference, which I have since heard was excellent—I spent most of my time on romantic walks in the woods, although I did manage to take in a couple sessions.

He eventually moved to where I live and we got married last fall. I did find out, though, that he mentioned me to his mother when we first started dating. His mother, out for a walk one day with a neighbor, was having a chat about how they'd like their sons to meet some nice girls. The neighbor, unaware of her walking partner's son's dating situation, suggested that he "go to the library and meet a nice girl." My now mother-in-law replied, "As a matter of fact, he did—the librarian!"

Al's[3] Story

I remember she wore a long-sleeved black sweater with a rolled collar and a straight, black skirt, a yellow mustard–colored trench coat draped over her arm. And her petite body floated by in freshman fluster past my desk, with her feet gliding softly on air. But, I, far too busy checking out books to notice, let her get almost past me before I asked her if I could be of help. And, as she filled out the white registration card, I do vaguely remember absently remarking on her hands, observing, I think, something about their having an unfinished quality about them.

Perhaps a casual eavesdropper might think I was politely expressing a gentlemanly interest in extending our chance meeting beyond mundane matters of library registration to loftier conversation. Yes, no doubt. I was, as many students were in those times, in a state of mild shock from near starvation (a condition I have fortunately extricated myself from since). I was penniless. My life was in a shambles. Would a young gentleman who had fallen on such hard times for one moment think it proper to burden a young lady with his company?

Recall, if you will, the days of the Renaissance and before. It was a widely held belief that the eyes are the windows to the soul. Other metaphysicians of the time felt a person's fate to be written in his countenance, complexion, and general facial features.

And for others schooled in the alchemy of the human soul, it is for them that the person's hands tell it all: the past, the present, and the future wishes of the subject. I refer not to the lines on the palms that gypsies read by campfire light in front of crystal balls, but rather to the shape of the hands themselves, a subject all who have studied sketching and the other fine arts will give testimony to, I am sure. Leonardo, bless him, and Raphael and Michelangelo too, all spent countless hours sketching, cartooning, and molding the likenesses of their many models' hands: the old, narrowed hands of the aging gardener; the hard, callous hands of the skilled carpenter; the confident, generous hands of the mother cleaning the child's scraped knee; the careless, disdaining hands of the countess, flipping back her hair and, in that same gesture, silently signaling her command to cut off the poor, unsuspecting duke's head.

Ah yes, her hands: young, slender, delicate, and gentle. Some people grow up quickly for whatever reasons, and their hands show a finality about them before their time. But hers, as I am reputed to have said, were wonderfully unfinished—filled with the dreamings of sweet youth. Hands are like the mind. They, too, learn, I believe. And like the mind, they too can close too soon and their digits become rigid, or they can stay open, supple, unfinished, wanting to learn and discover.

This, then, is what I saw that day as I—without guile or forethought of anything beyond that simple moment—absently gazed upon the fine lacework of her fingers and did so chance a casual observation about expansive vistas for her, yet to come.

I think that when we are at about the age of three, we understand all there is to understand. Then as we grow, consciousness blots from our minds those simple truths of childhood wisdom, which many of us then spend our lifetimes trying to recall. I think it is back then, around the gentle age of late infancy, that we first know what love is—not the love we have for the mother and father that protect and love us simply because we are—but that love the poets call true. Its nature is discovery and delight. As children we stumble upon true love as easily as we do upon the stairs, never calling it by name. And I think that as we grow, without knowing quite how or when it happened—we forget. Alas, the learning we must do to make us fit for living, by its very nature, makes this so. And then when we're all grown up, we meet the special person who causes that wonderful spark of recognition to flash. It is this special spark of beauty each beholds in his own eye in his own way, that spark which transcends our immediate time and the spot upon which we stand, transcends our public cultures, our private histories, our languages, and, most hopefully of all, the carefully laid plans of mice, men, and students working in the library. It is the spark of recognizing in the other person the presence of a childhood truth that was once ours—a recognition that calls us back to something we knew was true when we were but three years old.

Yes, the poets' true love, I think, is the act of being reunited with our own childhood. It is an experience that delights. True love is, I think, a kind of "thank-you" we say to the person who returns us to and then keeps returning us to that delight. And where do we glimpse these sparks? In a person's eyes? At the corner of her mouth? In her hands? I saw then on that fateful day in September many years ago, as I still see now, one such spark in those unfinished hands I still so love.

Joe's Story

I was a student reference assistant in the library at Trinity University, San Antonio, Texas, in 1966 and 1967. One day my wife-to-be came to the reference desk, where I was filling in while the reference librarian was away elsewhere, and asked a question (which, by the way, I was surprisingly able to answer). She was working on her thesis, which was about Bryan Callaghan, the last of the big boss mayors of San Antonio in the mid-1800s, as I recall. I helped her find something in the collection and after keeping my eye on her for a while, I saw her go to the circulation desk to check something out. After she left I hurried to the desk and commented to the student assistant on duty, "I need that woman's name and phone number."

I got it and called and asked her for a date. I was a student at St. Mary's University and was looking for a date for skip day. Everyone with a certain GPA didn't have to take finals in their last semester in school, and I was a senior. I was in that group and had planned to go to the Texas coast for the day with a friend of mine if I got a date.

I called Mary; we went to the coast and had a good time. I kept telling her that she needed to cover her back and legs or put on more lotion or she was going to get burned. She didn't pay any attention, saying that everything was okay. I should have known then what the future might hold. A week later, and for about a week, she looked horrible. All the skin on her back and legs had burned and was now peeling. In addition, from the day after we got back from the beach the pain resulting from a burn started.

On June 8, 1968, we got married in Vermillion, South Dakota. We have three children. About six years ago we took a family vacation on Lake Powell in Utah. Our daughter, who then was about twenty-one or so, didn't pay too much attention to the sun, which was shining all the time and was quite intense. She was told constantly by her mother, me, and others in the party that she needed to be careful about her legs burning. Like mother, like daughter. She didn't listen and burned her legs very badly, something that we now know can have serious health ramifications.

I still work in a library. We have had a good life with our three children, and are happy spending our days in each other's company.

For the Love of Information—Jason Bird

In 1996 I met the woman who would change my life, all because of two libraries. It was around 10:00 a.m. on a chilly Saturday morning in October that I arrived at the Leddy Library at the University of Windsor to work on a history paper. I thought myself quite eager for arriving so early and being so prepared for having this small but important assignment completed. This was due to the fact that I had recently missed a class for the reason we are not supposed to admit to in graduate school—I was out a little later than I had planned the night before. I also needed the notes for this class and saw a girl I knew from said class. She said to drop by her house, which was not far from mine, later in the day and she would give me her notes. When I went by she wasn't there, but her roommates were and they invited me in. I knew someone's boyfriend who was there, so we talked while everyone watched the Windsor Lancer football team being summarily destroyed. I started talking to one of the roommates, Suzanne. She was attractive and liked the same music I did, and she was from Burlington, which I considered part of Toronto—but she didn't appreciate that. But she didn't mind my rambling (I think she kind of does now) but I stayed as long as I could, and I had to see her again.

Two days later I was on my way to the library again and one of her roommates could tell there was a spark, at least from my side of the street, and she encouraged—virtually harassed—me to go back to their house and talk to Suzanne. I did and ended up walking her to school where I then asked her out for a drink, that night! After a little hesitation she said yes. After that night we started dating.

By the following summer we were so in love we didn't want to go home to our parents and be apart, as we lived only a few houses apart. We had mastered the art of calling our parents back in the morning and telling them we were just out at the gym, or something. My parents were notorious for calling at the earliest of hours; I think they just wanted to catch me! To stay together we took a summer class for the first two months, but then had to find jobs for July and August. Just before the end of June we both found work, at the same place. We were both hired through a federal grant to help reorganize (in other words, move) the collection of the Windsor Public Library. We informed WPL that we were going out but they didn't have a problem with it. For the first month everything was fine, as we were working with different people every day. But after a few weeks we ended up working together most of the time because we were told that together we worked more productively than any other group. This was great. Well, it was great until we ended up spending every single minute together. All of our friends were at home so we spent all of our free time with each other, walked to work together, ate together, did everything together.

By mid-August we were ready to kill each other; we were about to break up so we decided to give ourselves a break, but with our work schedule on a summer job this wasn't often possible. Thankfully just before her birthday we had a long weekend, so my parents came to visit and she went home to Burlington. I decided with the limited funds I had I would at least try to get her a romantic gift and take her out for her birthday when she got back.

We survived the summer, but barely. Thank God the job ended and we were able to get back to school!

A few years ago I was working in the corporate world and realized, although having learned a great deal there, that I was not helping anyone and I wasn't happy there. Someone asked me where, in a workplace, did I feel most comfortable, and strangely, it was at Windsor Public Library. With that, I left my corporate position in Toronto and went to the University of Western Ontario to get my MLIS and become a librarian. I am now a reference librarian and could never think of being in another field.

So I met my wife because I went to the library to study, and we almost broke up because we tried to work together in a library.

Ellen's[4] Story

I started work at sixteen as a library junior straight from school. In New Zealand during the 1970s it was possible to work and then gain an intermediate library qualification by a combination of distance and block courses without completing a degree. When I had been working for a whole two weeks I was introduced to a visiting journalist from out of town, who had worked as a student helper at this library before completing his training. This guy followed me around as I was shelving and tidying and insisted on telling me better ways to do the task, annoying me considerably as, after having helped in several school libraries on my travels as a "services brat," I thought that I did not require advice. In those days I was much shyer and too polite to tell someone that the more senior staff obviously liked the fact that having him looming over me, at 6'4" to my 5'3", was both irritating and a little intimidating. Luckily, one of the other staff noticed my discomfort and hauled him off, as I subsequently learned, to tell him off and tell him to take it easy on me, as I was very young.

Half an hour later he came bouncing back with a folded piece of paper and said he wanted my autograph. In the end, to get rid of him, I signed. "Tigger" then bounced away again, only to reappear about fifteen minutes later, demanding that I put my thumbprint on the document I had signed—only then would he let me read the piece of paper. Thoroughly curious and intrigued by now, I did so and then unfolded the paper to discover that I had been adopted and was now under "Tigger's" care. The document was "countersigned by the Town

Clock and City Mare [*sic*]." I promptly fell blissfully in love and spent the next few months in a spin of frequent letters and infrequent dates. We could only get together occasionally, as he worked in another city over a hundred miles away.

Our romance did come to an end soon after, due to a misunderstanding on my part, but I never forgot and never found anyone else who was able to make me feel quite as special. We've kept in touch on and off over the years; New Zealand is a small country and it's quite easy to find people when you know roughly where they are. We are both the sort of people who love trivia and general knowledge and will occasionally phone one another when we want to run down a fact or story. And thirty-odd years later I'd still check him out and take him home if he hadn't already been borrowed by another avid reader.

Notes

1. *Edmonton Journal*, July 10, 2004, A1. Used with permission.
2. Used with permission.
3. Pseudonym.
4. Pseudonym.

CHAPTER SIX

The Romance of
Academic Libraries

Before I went to graduate school I spent a year working as a library assistant in a departmental library of a large research university. I hadn't been mentally ready to leave university after my undergraduate degree, and I was quite envious of the senior and graduate students who spent their days in the library. I felt a subtle barrier between them and myself, even though we were about the same age. A very traditional library, it had the feel of a gentlemen's club, with its long mahogany tables, brass lamps, and leather chairs. I soaked up the atmosphere every day, considering myself very fortunate to be working there, even if my salary was a pittance. I frequently met the authors of the standard works I had used during my undergraduate days.

One particular group of students came to the library almost every day. They were a cheerful, laughing crowd. Gradually they welcomed me into their group, and I started having coffee and sometimes going to plays and movies with them (to the disapproval of the chief librarian who considered fraternizing with patrons a sin). They were all from the same college of the university, working with the same professor. One day he came in and I was introduced. He had the aura of a star about him. He dressed in a very trendy manner for the times (the 1970s), quite unlike all the tweed-jacketed professors who were library regulars. I was instantly smitten. What clinched it was the articulated silver fish he wore on a long chain around his neck. As a Piscean, I was captivated.

In the ensuing months, the professor continued to be friendly toward me, inviting me to join his coffee chats with his students. Looking back I believe he had a faint air of amusement about him, no doubt because my heart was firmly visible on my sleeve. I was happy with my romantic daydreams and cherished no hopes of anything more, as I had met his wife, also a star professor, who occasionally used the library too. As summer approached, I began to feel pangs at the thought of leaving the library as my contract drew to a close. That group of students was also about to disperse. Their professor and his wife threw a large garden party at their lovely house in the country, and to my joy I was invited.

I spent hours preparing for the big day, wanting to look my best. Memories of it are hazy now, although I know I had a wonderful time. As I was about to leave, knowing that I probably wouldn't see most of these people again, I went to thank my hosts. The professor smiled at me and said, "I thought you would like this as a keepsake," and handed me the fish necklace. I wore it every day for months.

Academic libraries have long been a place for romance between a staff member and a patron, even though many contacts told me that they worked under an unwritten rule that there was to be no personal relationship between the two. From the accounts I received, however, when it became clear that something special might be going on, all thoughts of rules were given low priority. Even in a place of learning, it seems, the heart can often rule the head.

Maryon's Story

My long-time partner picked me up when I worked in the periodicals reading room at the University of Alberta. He used to come to the reading room to request back files of the Mexican newspaper *El Día*. I must admit I'd been watching him and felt some electricity in the room before I'd even see him. After several weeks of requesting the newspapers, one of my colleagues told me she was seeing him regularly at the swimming pool and he was saying hello to her. I thought I'd lost out to my attractive blonde friend! But, the next Friday night when I was scheduled to work until 6:00 p.m. and close the reading room, guess who happened to be working late and asked for my phone number as I was about to make the closing announcement? After that, I was always the one who offered to go into the storage area to get the old issues of *El Día*—and he often offered to come with me and help to retrieve them. That was twenty-five years ago.

Jerry's Story

I was the supervisor on the evening shift of the circulation/reserve reading desk in the agricultural campus library of a large Big Ten university. A new student worker caught my eye as she made her way from the circulation desk to the photocopy machine. It wasn't just her form-fitting red sweater and the form it fit, it was the resoluteness of her march to the machine—as if she would walk through walls if any were in the way of providing what the customer needed. A couple days later, as I was searching for a place to have lunch in the student center, I saw her sitting alone in a cafeteria booth. I couldn't pass on the opportunity! I sidled over and said, "Mind if I join you?" "No," she replied somewhat hesitantly. I turned on what little Irish charm I could muster, attempting to develop some sort of interest on her part. Forty-five minutes of nothing. I chalked it up as just one more strikeout.

Months later, I was having lunch with several friends in the same student center. The conversation turned to movies and who were the actors who played each of the main roles in "The Magnificent Seven." We were stuck at six. Stumped, we headed, en masse, for the library where, behind the desk, sat my erstwhile lunch partner with the cold shoulder. Having never been one to hold a grudge, I explained our predicament. She immediately came up with the missing Brad Dexter, and as a kicker, informed us that Eli Wallach was not one of the seven and that we had, in error, included him instead of Robert Vaughn. How could any aspiring reference librarian not fall in love with a "garbage head" like that?

It took me two years of persevering as she worked her way through a couple of other boyfriends, but we wound up together in library school and married just in time for me to do most of the work on her master's degree paper based on a user survey of the library where I had recently been employed.

Barbara's Story

While filling in at the circulation desk one day, I entered into our computer system a new community borrower. I noticed his unusual first name of Jacobus and made a comment about how nice the name was. One thing led to another and after several checkout conversations (in more ways than one) we went on a date. That was seven years ago and we have been happily married for three of them.

John's Story

I met and fell in love with a wonderful young woman working at a university library where I am employed. Sadly, it did not work out in the long run. I started working at the library in the fall of 2000. A nice young woman caught my attention, but I was always too shy to get the courage up to talk with her. I remember seeing her in the library, by the photocopiers, and talking with her every now and then. It was finally about a year or so later that we talked more regularly. She told me she was in the Ph.D. program in English. She was a teaching assistant and was taking graduate classes.

I remember our first official date was going to see a play, *The Lonesome West* by Martin McDonagh. I read a review of it in our local paper and mentioned it to her. She came by the library, checked out the newspaper, read the same article, and mentioned that it would be nice to go together. I bought tickets for a Friday night performance. However, a day or so before the play she said she would like to go to a poetry reading that same night, and asked if I could exchange the tickets. I was able to switch them to Saturday night, so we went to a lecture and poetry reading on Friday, and dinner and a play on Saturday night. It was a wonderful weekend. Over the next several months we would see each other in the library and chat, mostly small talk, and say hi and smile to each other. I found out that she enjoyed Irish literature and music, and was studying for her French language exam. She told me that she too had started at the university in the fall of 2000. By the fall of 2002 we had met for coffee and lunch a few times, and we exchanged names and numbers and e-mail addresses.

In March of 2003 I took a trip to Ireland. My friend had dropped off a travel book about Ireland and had jotted down a few nice places to visit in Dublin. During the spring and summer we spent a lot of time together. I knew I was truly and genuinely in love with her. I remember checking out some videos and CDs for her, and also remember helping her with a small word processor that the library had. We had so many nice talks, and started to get to know each other better. She told me where she was from originally and I told her my hometown was Freeport, Illinois. During one summer, she actually worked part time in the archives department in the library, and I remember seeing her in the staff lounge making tea and coffee, saying hi and smiling.

We started to date and would often say hello when we saw each other in the library. During the last year or so, we spent more and more time together. When she moved to a new apartment, I helped her by collecting some empty boxes from the library. It was a busy time of year, the fall semester had just started, and the university had recently opened up a new library which was very nice and also very busy.

The last year or so, we were dating, talking, meeting for coffee at a little coffee shop in the library. She would come by my work area and we'd go out for lunch, and a few nights when she taught night classes we would go out for dinner and I would drive her home.

We really got to know each other, met each other's families and friends, and had a lot of good times. We had arguments and disagreements as well. After one disagreement, she dropped off a note for me at the library saying she was sorry. However, I guess it was not just meant to be. I think it is a little bit of unrequited love. So much of literature is filled with unrequited love, of love lost. I met and fell in love with a special, wonderful young woman working in a university library. It just didn't work out, for whatever reason, although I guess it is better to have loved and lost, rather than not to have loved at all.

My Library Romance—Barb Carr

In the fall of 1988, I was working as a librarian at St. Lawrence College in Kingston, Ontario. Things were a little chaotic, since we were in the middle of automating the library, and I had just come back from a six-month management stint at our Brockville Campus.

One of my responsibilities was to schedule library tours, which were conducted by the library technicians and the two librarians. Toward the end of September, a new part-time English teacher, David Craig, came to the library to arrange library tours for two evening classes—his and that of a fellow teacher. The other, more seasoned, teacher had suggested to David that it would be a good time for the students to visit the library and asked David to take care of it. The challenge for the library was in handling two classes (which we usually split into small groups) in the same evening, when we normally had just two library staff on duty. In this case, the classes were fairly small, so I thought one tour group per class would work fine, and booked the two tours for David. However, one of the library technicians who would be working that evening informed me that she was not comfortable leading tours, and in fact would not do so. I suggested that she see if one of the other technicians would take the tour for her. I wasn't optimistic that this would happen, so I decided we would have to amalgamate the groups, and contacted David to ask that both classes come at the same time as one tour group. Later, after mulling it over, I realized one tour group just wouldn't work for the combined number of students, so I decided I would have to come in and take one of the groups myself. I contacted David yet again, to say we were back to two groups. As it happened, one of the other library technicians had agreed to cover for the one not doing tours, so there were actually three tour guides available for the two classes on the evening they visited the library!

With all this scheduling and rescheduling of tours, David certainly knew who I was by the time the students actually got to the library— and probably thought I was completely disorganized! However, in the days after the tours, I noticed that David was still dropping by the library to borrow books, and would always stop by for a chat if I were at the reference desk. One day we were in the middle of a rather eso-teric chat about Roland Barthes (in a Woody Allen film there would have been subtitles with our actual thoughts), when I noticed that a small line was forming at the reference desk. I told David I had to go and help them, but that I would like to continue the conversation, and maybe we could have coffee sometime? To my delight, he was in the library first thing the next morning to find out when my coffee break was! Two years later, we were married.

Heidi's Story

To help put myself through university, I worked in the university library computer center, where I was introduced to the Internet. I met my husband online. I later moved on to other departments in the library, but when I was working the early morning shift, I'd have access to a computer and we'd chat in between the few and far between patrons. Eventually we got married, and I had to transfer libraries!

Julia's Story

I was in library school at Emory University in 1976. During my second quarter, I took a class in government documents. The first day of the class, the professor gave a rambling philosophical lecture about why we study (or why people use) government information, a rather cosmic view of people and their quest for information. At the close of his lecture, he said something like, "So the reason we study government documents is because we all want love." The professor also mentioned, early on, that he didn't like to assign grades and that we would be asked to grade our own performance at the end of the quarter.

I found the course subject matter difficult, but trudged dutifully several times each week to the ground level of the Woodruff Library, where the government documents section was located at that time. Observing my frustration after several visits, the library worker on duty—an attractive man—approached me and asked if I needed some assistance. Of course I did, and from that point on I timed my government documents visits with his work schedule. He was a huge help!

Pretty soon he asked me to take his dinner break with him, and shortly thereafter asked for a date. We fell in love quickly. By the end of the quarter it was clear that the relationship was serious.

The professor scheduled an end-of-course conference with each student, to determine the student's grade, among other things. I told the professor I had no qualms about giving myself an A—because I had found love. He agreed.

As soon as I finished my degree in December 1976, I married the government documents specialist. We are still married, with two kids, almost twenty-eight years later.

Ruby's Story

It has been fifteen years since my husband, Mohan Pal, passed away and yet it also seems like only yesterday that we met at the University of Toronto Library. We met at the circulation desk.

The year was 1965 and we were both immigrants of Indian origin living in Toronto, Canada. He had come from Munich, Germany, after working there for a few years to study engineering in Canada. I, on the other hand, had come to finish my library science degree at the University of Toronto. Mohan came to know my name through a couple who knew me from my time way back in the early sixties in the United States. I had gone there to study and get some practical experience in my field. Since we both belonged to the same religion, spoke the same language, and had similar social backgrounds, Mohan became curious about me and decided that he wanted to have a look at the girl whom he had heard so much of from mutual friends.

I can still vividly recall the day he came to the university library, pretending to borrow a book, and asked for me by name. I used to work in the serials department at that time. My supervisor called and informed me that somebody at the circulation desk was looking for me. I went out and saw him standing there with a book in his hand. He was tall, handsome, and looking very smart in a nice suit with a great smile on his face. He introduced himself and mentioned the names of our common friends and wasted no time in inviting me to lunch that very same afternoon.

The next few days were spent in seeing each other regularly and getting to know each other very well. Even though I had been enamored from the first day, I did not want to express my feelings for him too quickly and I waited until I could sense that he was feeling the same way.

Soon afterward he sent a letter to his parents in India asking for their permission to marry me. They were overjoyed upon reading the good news that he had found a Bengali girl in Canada with whom he could settle and they consented happily.

We first met on June 1, 1965; he proposed to me a few days later on June 6 at Toronto Centre Island and we got married July 15, 1965, at the old Toronto City Hall. It was a whirlwind affair!

We were very happily married for twenty-four years and I have two wonderful boys to carry on his name. They love and take care of me just like their father had done. I, indeed, feel so fortunate to have them and to be their mother. So, for all the people out there, be ready! Romance can strike anywhere—even at a library!

Amy's[1] Story

In September 2001, I started working as a business and law librarian at a college. At around the same time, Bill[2] started his LLB degree at the college. Students were always encouraged to come and ask for help if they needed it and Bill was one of those people who came into my office quite frequently to ask for assistance with finding law material. I liked Bill from the start: apart from being very attractive, he was polite and had a friendly face and a kind way about him. He always left me with a warm, positive feeling. At the time, I wasn't all that aware of the attraction. I had been through some difficult relationships and wasn't interested in looking for anyone.

It wasn't until the second year that my feelings for Bill began to intensify—to the point where I started to behave like a love-struck teenager. My work colleagues would even call me in the office to let me know when my law student was in the library! I drove them mad because I just couldn't pluck up the courage to ask the student out!

Toward the end of the second year I had to teach library skills to some law dissertation students. Bill was one of the few students who showed up—I could have died when I saw him there. I didn't think I could stand up and teach him feeling the way I did, but I got through it. After the session, I set the students up with a password to get into some databases. Bill chose a young girl's name and at that point I convinced myself that he was happily married with kids and that I had no chance. It was pointless.

Time passed and because I hadn't seen Bill for a while, I thought I had gotten over him. On a Friday in April 2004, he walked into my office once more. All of the feelings came flooding back. I helped him find a book and fell over my words completely as I spoke to him. My excuse was that I was all over the place trying to do my boss's job while he was away. Bill remarked, "If it is any consolation, you are a lot better looking than your boss." I thanked him and felt my stomach do a somersault in his presence. When he left, a colleague asked if there was something going on between us because the student was taking a lot of interest in my work. It got me thinking.

Over the weekend, I made up my mind I had to do something. I had found out that Bill only had three weeks before he finished his degree and I knew I couldn't let him slip away. Knowing that he would have to bring his book back into the library on the Monday morning, I raced into work that day fully psyched up to ask him out. I almost backed out—but a colleague pushed me in his direction.

It was probably one of the hardest things I have ever done. My body and voice trembled as I asked Bill for a few minutes of his time. We perched ourselves on the edge of the service desk and then I asked if there wasn't already someone in his life, would he like to go for a drink with me after work? He just smiled nodding, saying he was really flattered—over and over. Then he said, "But there is someone."

I couldn't get rid of him quick enough—I wanted to run and hide under a desk! As he walked away, I blurted out that it took a lot out of me to do that. He turned round and said, "Well, you never know." What on earth did that mean? I tried not to hang on those words too much, but couldn't really help it.

The next day, Bill came back into the office, but I was in the staff room and wasn't going to come out. I was too embarrassed. The next three days I was away at a conference.

On the following Tuesday, Bill came walking toward me while I was on the information desk with a colleague. He said that he'd been thinking about our last conversation and everything was okay: he would like to get to know me and would I like to go out for the drink after all? I turned round and said that I didn't think it would be right if he was seeing someone. He asked if that was a no on my part and I answered that if he was seeing someone, then it was a no.

I could tell that Bill wanted to run away, just as I had wanted to the previous week. I told him that I wanted everything to be okay and for him to still ask for help if he needed it. He agreed that nothing would change and then sped away.

I turned to my colleague and asked him if I really said no to this guy that I had liked for three years! I couldn't believe what I had done—I kicked myself. At the same time, I felt that I had done the right thing and that it wouldn't have been right to go out with someone knowing they were already involved with someone else.

Afterward, I couldn't get Bill out of my head (again)! I decided that perhaps it would be acceptable to go out for a coffee on campus. After all, I didn't know his circumstances and he was leaving so it would be easy enough to stop anything from happening. I saw him the next day and went straight up to him. I completely forgot what I had planned to say and stumbled over my words again, but managed to ask him out for a coffee. I said that it would be "acceptable" at the same time Bill said that it would be "safe"—our words overlapped.

We arranged to meet up on a Thursday because he had a six-year-old daughter whom he would have to collect on Friday. He was late for our meeting due to a presentation he had to give for college—but that didn't matter. In the short time we had, we connected in so many ways.

We went out on a proper date a couple of weeks later and discovered that we had a lot in common—we both liked horror movies, similar music, and were both at similar stages in our lives. We talked deeply about many things that people generally don't touch upon on a first date. I found out that Bill was seeing someone, but in his words, it wasn't a bed of roses. Fortunately, she wasn't the mother of his child—his daughter was from a marriage that had ended a long time ago. After he completed all of his exams, he ended the relationship with the other person. We both agreed it would be more sensible to wait until then and it also gave us time to get to know each other as friends first.

At the end of the day, I wasn't what broke them up—but I perhaps gave Bill the push he needed to face the fact that the relationship had reached its natural end. It transpired that he liked me all along too and had wanted to ask me out but thought I was engaged because of a ring I wore on my left hand. He had also been thinking about me a lot over that weekend after we saw each other in the library. The timing was perfect—if I had asked him out a year earlier as I had wanted to, it wouldn't have been the right time for either of us.

We have been together about seven months now and are very happy. Some would call this the honeymoon period, but we are both very optimistic about our future together. We still talk about our tug-of-war situation when we got together and how it was simply meant to be. We both believe that fate had a hand in bringing us together.

Notes

1. Pseudonym.
2. Pseudonym.

CHAPTER SEVEN

The Romance of Public Libraries

I received more accounts of romance in public libraries than any other type. They also seem to be the most likely setting for romance to be sparked between a staff member and a patron. Romance seems to occur in all kinds of public libraries, from the monumental New York Public Library to the smallest rural branch.

The Englewood Public Library in New Jersey was the scene of romance for two well-known senior citizens. Hy Eisman is the cartoonist for *Popeye* and *Katzenjammer Kids* comic strips. He was widowed in 1997. The counselor of his support group urged him to initiate a conversation with a stranger in a public place. In the library he spotted Florenz Greenberg. He was too nervous to say much but handed her his business card and left.

Florenz Greenberg, also widowed in 1997, is the managing editor at CavanKerry Press in Fort Lee, New Jersey. A few weeks after their meeting at the library, she came across his card and decided to do a Web search on him as an exercise for her newly acquired Internet skills. She called him, thrilled she had found the information she was looking for. Their first movie date was an outing to the animited movie *Antz*. They rapidly realized they had much in common and a romance ensued. In 2004, they sent out comic strip invitations to their wedding, with details courtesy of Popeye and Olive Oyl. The wedding was featured in The *New York Times*.[1]

Paul's Story

About twelve years ago, I was living in New York City and worked for the New York Public Library at Lincoln Center in the music division. As a musician with a Ph.D. but without a library degree, I was a subject specialist, but worked in reference and technical services. It was spring-time, and during one of my morning desk shifts, a patron came up to the desk and asked me if I could help her to use the online catalog, CATNYP. She explained she was looking for Jewish music, but couldn't find anything in the catalog. We walked over to a terminal, I showed her how to make a subject search, and asked her if there was a particu-lar aspect of Jewish music she wanted, to limit the thousands of results we had. She explained she was a singer/guitarist looking for certain kinds of songs. She had an accent, so curiously I asked her where she was from; she told me she was from Paris, and was in New York making a few performances. I explained to her how to request the items she wanted and she went off to look at her books and music scores. My shift finished, I had lunch, and I spent most of the afternoon doing technical services work. As I was leaving the office for the day, I noticed the patron I had helped in the morning was just passing through the security check, so I decided to make my way down the hall slowly enough that we would take the elevator together.

When we met again at the elevator, she thanked me for my help and said that she appreciated the material I helped her find. We began to chat a little and introduced ourselves: her name was Hélène (how typically French, I thought). I asked about the music she sang, and I boldly explained I was a guitarist. She wasn't totally uninterested in knowing that, and as we walked toward the subway (she was heading south to the village, I north to Washington Heights) we exchanged numbers. She was returning to France in three weeks, and we met a few times casually, but it was during her last week in New York we discov-ered ourselves in a fairly romantic situation.

After she left, we wrote almost every day, spoke on the phone at least weekly, and after a month, I decided to take a few weeks off work and fly to Paris in June. That was the beginning of a transatlantic rela-tionship that very quickly became an engagement, and we were married in New York in January, about nine months after we had met. I decided to pursue the MLIS to continue a serious career in librarianship, we moved to Montréal later that year so I could I attend McGill University, and we've been here since then, now with two wonderful young boys. And I still have to explain to her how to search online. Who says you can't find romance in the library!

Janette's Story

I have worked in libraries for nearly twelve years, just over five of these at my current library. I met my husband here while I was working one evening on the reference desk. I was working closely with the young adult programming and collection and building connections with the local schools. One Thursday evening in October 1999, a teacher from one of the middle schools came in and needed *Hatchet* by Gary Paulsen on cassette to use in his seventh grade reading class. We discussed working together on future reading lists and other collaboration as well as the upcoming Teen Read Week. I thought, "Wow, a handsome middle school reading teacher who uses the public library."

Over the next few months, we talked a few times over the phone about authors or titles for his class. However, I hadn't seen him since that one night. Then all of a sudden, there he was. On a Sunday afternoon in February 2000, he came to the reference desk with one of his friends who needed help with some research. Shortly after they left, Steve called me at the reference desk because he had meant to ask about a new reading list—then he asked me out. We were engaged that summer and married in November 2000. Since then, we have had a beautiful child of our own which compliments the child we each had of our own. Our girls (ten months apart) are the best friends I have ever seen. What used to be a quiet family of one parent and one daughter, is now a wonderful home full of the life and energy of two parents and three great children (of course the golden retriever, Buddy, loves all the food the toddler will share).

Anna's Story

I met my husband in the public library. He was in law school and researching boundary law for a professor. He was checking sites on historic maps and he had to fill out request slips to pull the maps from our secure files. With his idiosyncratic handwriting, it took me two days to decipher that he was signing Mickey Mouse and Donald Duck on the forms. Naturally, when he asked me out on a date, I had to accept. Thirty-five years later, we are still together, mostly because I am a patient, tolerant person!

Janine's Story

Jim and I met in 1997 at the Walnut Grove Library where I had just started working. Jim was looking for something to read and I suggested a number of titles that he might be interested in. Weeks, months, and a few years went by with me doing this and him asking if I'd like to go for coffee. We'd sit at the little cafe inside the community center where the library was located and have coffee and occasionally lunch. When the *Harry Potter* books became the popular titles they are, I was enjoying them so much, I recommended them to him. When the first movie came out we had talked about going to see it together, but it just didn't work out. In September of 2002, I applied for another job within the library system, but in a different location, and was accepted. Jim came in on my last day and asked for my phone number. Knowing I was leaving he decided he needed to do something if he wanted to see me ever again. He came to see me a few times in my new location, and when the second *Harry Potter* movie came out in November 2002 we went on our first official date. In January of 2004 we got engaged and on July 17, 2004, we were married.

Marianne's Story

I'm a librarian and met, fell in love with, and married my husband at the public library where I work. He was one of our security officers. We both had gone through divorces at the same time and formed a friendship. Finally one day we decided to take it one step further and went out to dinner on a date. That led to a wonderful relationship that grew into love. Jim proposed to me at the reference desk with a dozen roses and an engagement ring hidden inside. Six months later we were married in our library's reading room. It's a beautiful room built around

1936 with a wonderful fireplace, a two-story-high ceiling and recessed bookshelves. We cleared the room of its furniture and set up seats in rows to form an aisle for my dad to walk me down. The fireplace was decorated with a garland of flowers. It couldn't have been more romantic. The library was the basis for our whole relationship.

Andrea's Story

My husband Jim and I met at the Vogelson branch of the Camden County Library in Voorhees, New Jersey. I was working as a library assistant in circulation and he was a seasonal maintenance worker as well as a security guard. We were celebrating a fellow coworker's retirement with a get-together before the library opened. In the children's department, where part of the party was, there was a couch. I sat on the couch and broke it. At that time I was only 105 pounds so it was amazing that I broke a couch. Out came my future husband as maintenance worker to take the couch away. He said something to me about how could I have possibly broken the couch. That was our first encounter. Later that day he was working in security and it was our annual book sale. I saw him, he saw me, and we started talking. The rest is history. We were friends for about a year, dated, then got engaged and married, all while we were still at the library. He became head of security, and then moved into a job in our technical services department. I went to get my MLS and became a children's librarian at the same library. We had both of our children while we worked there. We even had a joint bridal and baby shower given by our coworkers at the library. My husband has now moved to a different job in the county. I'm still in the children's department.

It Happened in the Library—Jeff[2]

Things change yet somehow remain the same. . . . I met her in a library one rainy Saturday morning. I was there haunting the many tomes of fiction and she was there as a trainee for the library. It was dark in an unused portion of the library, with chairs stacked on tables in storage and only the light she carried chased the shadows away. For some reason totally innocent, we found ourselves together there. We touched and kissed as strangers and the moment solidified us forever. I was the kind that you never brought home to mother and a rebel and she was the gentle flower that got caught up in the moment. We both knew our destinies were off in different directions and could never be together although deep down things had changed in how we would see each other forever.

I went off into the world and she continued at her tasks. We started our communications prior to the advent of the Internet and many letters chased me around. I returned them almost the same day I received them. Finally around thirty-five years later, after staying in touch sporadically now via e-mail, we again met and reacquainted ourselves with the many paths our lives had taken. The time had not dimmed our friendship nor had it lessened in intensity as we shared a coffee, a kiss, and a laugh. I had gone off into the world as a man with many good and bad adventures with many different names and a shadow existence and she now was the head of the libraries here and had as well a myriad of municipal duties.

I am here again, now as a private investigator doing what I have done for thirty-odd years all over, only now back here where I started. Chance and many tragedies have tossed me again on this shore that I had secretly sworn never to return to. As for my librarian friend, she still calls me by a name long buried in the past and is editing my first novel and helping me to sort it out for publishing. She was there in the beginning and will be there forever as my dearest closest friend. Time whistled by and changed the entire landscape, moment by moment, but something as innocent as a kiss with a stranger in a library has made many positive changes in my life. I was always the blind one, and she was my guide all along though time and space lay between us and eventually put us back in arm's reach once more, with her again as a mentor of sorts and me as a budding author in her territory. We still kiss and hug when we meet: between us will always be that stormy afternoon in that dark storage room where a kiss started it all.

No names were mentioned because we both must retain our secrets from coworkers—but she knows who she is, and the influence she had—forever a friend, never a lover, and never to know how much she is loved.

I Married My Librarian—The Reverend
Dr. Michael J. J. Collier

In 1971, I quit grade twelve, got a job, and moved into Halifax. A lifelong reader, I went to the library headquarters for books. One young woman there usually served me. She always smiled and showed genuine interest in my subject area—religion and spirituality. I knew nothing about her and had *no* romantic interests; I intended to become a monk. I learned later that she had no desire whatsoever to marry a clergyman. But, I did like her friendly manner and thought she'd make a wonderful Christian, so I began to pray for her!

Unbeknownst to me, she had noted my reading interests and was praying for me in the same vein. In fact, she even prayed that it would be nice if I could meet someone like a certain youth leader who might help me in my spiritual quest.

As Providence had it, the next time we saw each other, I had not only met that chap, but he and I were visiting her church for a joint youth meeting. She was the organist, though at first, I wasn't quite sure it was her as this was the first time I ever saw her *not* smiling! When the service was over, we dashed to the back, startling everyone because we obviously knew each other, though the congregational "gatekeepers" didn't know *me*!

Three months later my friend and I were attending my librarian's church for completely unrelated reasons. Then, for fellowship only—not romantic interest—she and I agreed to attend a Valentine's Day banquet together. Much to both our surprise, we dated on Monday and Tuesday, got engaged on Wednesday, and then got elected king and queen of the Sweetheart Banquet on Friday—the others were just being nice and didn't know we had even dated yet! Five months later—thirty-two years ago this summer—we were married! I went on to get my education and become a clergyman, just not a monk!

Not only did we both read religious topics, we each prayed for the other to be a Christian. She married her pastor (something she'd never wanted to do!) and I married my librarian! Perhaps the moral of the story is: "Watch what you read!" Or maybe it's "Watch what you pray for; you might get something you're not expecting!"

Neil's Story

I'm the branch head of the Bruce Hutchison Library, a branch of the Greater Victoria Public Library on Vancouver Island. One day I received one of those phone calls from a friend which I suspect most librarians get from time to time, and if they're like me, they don't like them much. They go like this: "Hi, we're setting up a library in our office/church/etc. . . . And could you tell us how to do it?" Preferably, they'd like you to do it over the phone and in less than ten minutes.

I stifled the urge to ask her if she ever phones her doctor and asks him to help her with an appendectomy over the phone. Instead, I launched into my usual spiel about libraries being very complex entities which are best organized by professional librarians, and suggested that they might want to hire a bright library school student for the task.

My friend eventually realized that her library wasn't going to be organized with a phone call. But, she persisted and asked if someone from her office could drop by and chat. I agreed and hoped that in person I could convince them to employ a librarian.

Kim walked promptly into the library the following day, wearing a blue pin-striped suit and a confident, serious expression when we met at the reference desk. I showed her around the library and we began to chat about the mysteries of classification, indexing, and authority control.

After about half an hour I was very convinced that not only could Kim set up a library, but she could probably lead a Central American coup and run a small- to medium-sized country with little or no help. As she prepared to leave, I was surprised to hear myself asking if she'd like to have a glass of wine together some time.

Well, that was a few years ago now. The wallpaper on the reference desk computer I'm writing this on shows a picture of our cheerful, happy son Jack who is nearing his second birthday.

There's one other interesting twist in this amorous tale. I vividly remember the first time I approached this same reference desk. I was a new librarian with the Greater Victoria Public Library and wanted to introduce myself to the various branch and department heads. If you'd told me then that not only would I be sitting in the branch head's chair on the other side of the desk, where I'd meet my future wife, but that the branch head I met that day would one day be a godparent to our son, well, I'd have said you were dreaming.

Suzanne's Story

In the spring of 1968 I was working in the social science department of the Los Angeles Public Library on a busy Saturday when a young man asked for help and then started to flirt with me. I thought he would ask me out but then he disappeared. About a half hour later when it had quieted down he came up to the desk and handed me a note asking me if I would go out with him. He said he hadn't wanted to get turned down in front of the previous crowd. I had a policy of not going out with customers, but I decided to break that policy and take a chance on him.

Our wedding took place in November of 1968 and we have celebrated more than thirty-six years of marriage.

Connie's Story

My husband and I have been married for more than twenty-four years, and our courtship took place in the Niagara Falls Public Library. Kyle and I attended the same high school, where he dated one of my best friends for several years. For various reasons, I never thought of him as potential date or boyfriend material. After high school we headed off to different universities, and Kyle and my girlfriend stopped seeing each other. Five and a half years later I was working as a library assistant on the reference desk at Niagara Falls Public Library. Kyle returned from Australia where he had completed his master's degree. He began to spend long hours in the library working on his master's thesis. We struck up a friendship, which led to my editing his thesis, and our eventual courtship.

The library staff, many of whom were elderly and unmarried, was very interested in the development of our relationship, especially since my future husband tended to show up at the library after playing ball hockey, wearing his tattered ball hockey clothes. What could I possibly see in this disheveled young man? And weren't they surprised after they called police due to a problematic patron and Kyle arrived alongside the police officer? Kyle was in uniform—as an auxiliary (volunteer) police officer.

A year and a half later we were married, with many of my library colleagues in attendance at the church. I have said more than once over the years that libraries are ideal places to meet that someone special.

Andrea's Story

When I was sixteen years old, I always went to the library on Fridays with my father. In the library was a section for comic books. These comic books were in boxes on the wall instead of on the usual bookshelves, so the section was very narrow. One Friday I made eye contact with someone there.

The next Friday he was there again and we made eye contact again. Because it was a narrow space it was the beginning of a conversation. But because I was with my father I had to go. We agreed to meet the next week. On that occasion we gave each other our phone numbers (the cell phone wasn't on the market yet) and I waited for his phone call. He was my first boyfriend but it didn't last long. I was very young.

Last year I met him again in a club/bar. It was eleven years later, but it was love at second sight. It didn't work out, but everything has its reasons. We both needed each other when we met again. Now we are very good friends. He will always have a special place in my heart, and when I enter the library sometimes I have to smile at the comics section.

The library is in Enschede, The Netherlands.

A LUV Story—Mike Madigan

It happened at the library one spring when I was just seven years old. An encyclopedia caught my eye although at the time I didn't know it was an encyclopedia. All I saw was volume three and the title was placed vertically:

HOW
to
LUV

The titles of the similar books before and after it didn't seem to make sense. Volume one said:

AAA
to
DLO

while volume four possessed the title that said:

LUW
to
PIQ

But somehow that title HOW to LUV caught my eye because, yes, even though I was only seven years old, I had fallen in love with a very cute girl I had seen who often went into the library to read quietly. I was fascinated by her looks and even though you might find it hard to believe one so young could be in love, I was madly in love. It was my first reason to ever want to explore a library and, had the old librarian really known my intentions, I don't think she would have had me there. Of course when I went to take out this book the librarian said, "Oh no, Michael, you can't take out this book. It's an encyclopedia and it's from the reserve section."

"Oh," I said sadly.

"What are you looking for?" she asked me curiously.

Now I was speechless. I stammered, "I . . . I . . . I'm not really sure. Just a book. I'll put this back," I said, feeling my face flush red.

That was years ago. Ever notice there are still some things we can think back about that make us blush even to this day?

As for the girl I was madly in love with? We did go out once years later in high school. Looks aren't everything.

Alan's Story

I guess my earliest romantic experience (or lack of it) was when I fell in love with the young children's librarian named Jean Squirrel. I went to the library every day, and decided there and then that I would (a) become a librarian and (b) marry Jean Squirrel and have lots of little literate nutkins. Alas it was not to be, because a few years later, before I could start working at the library, she married and changed her name to Scragg. Things were never the same once the Squirrel became a Scragg, but I did become a librarian.

Nina's Story

I met my husband in the Greenville Carnegie Library. He was an experimental aircraft pilot, rode Harley Davidson motorcycles, and played the guitar. He just couldn't get my mind off my empty stomach long enough to get me interested in him.

My goal was to become a librarian. My main goal was not realized by me but by my daughter, Lisa. My first job though, after graduating from St. Louis Christian College, was in Greenville Carnegie Library, where I met my husband. The day I began as a library clerk, the woman in charge of the desk in the main lobby of Carnegie Library cornered me, shaking her finger in my face and declaring, "This is no place for a young woman to work. The only men you meet in the library are old married men who are too cheap to buy their own newspapers or single-minded men who can't get their noses out of a book long enough to notice you're a woman!"

What she didn't realize was I was desperate to work at any job to earn enough money to be able to move out of my parents' house. Marriage was not in my plans at the moment. Or maybe she was worried I wanted her job?

"Just mark my words," she said, sniffing and stomping back to the main desk.

Not long after this, it became my turn to relieve her from her main desk duty so she could have a lunch break. I assumed by her attitude that this was to be a great honor for me, to be allowed into her realm. Honestly, all I could think about was how hungry I was. *I hope she isn't late getting back. The book cart is full of returned books. I guess I can sort them so they will be easier to shelve.*

"Excuse me. Could you help me?" A masculine voice seeped into my reverie.

"Yes. What do you need?" I turned to look into the bluest eyes of a very engaging young man. He had the nicest smile.

"Could you tell me where the motorcycle books are?"

"Yes. They are located in the nonfiction section of the stacks right through that door to your right beyond the photocopier."

I returned to the book cart and sorted some more books. *Wonder what Mom packed in my lunch?*

"Excuse me again. I'm not sure my library card is up to date. Can I still check out books?"

Oh bother. Where is the desk supervisor? "Tell me your name. I'll check your card status."

"I'm Philip Leibfacher." He smiled so wide I declare he could have doubled for the Cheshire Cat.

"And you spell that how?"

"Philip has one L, as P-H-I-L-I-P. The last name is spelled L-E-I, B as in brilliant, then F as in fantastic, A-C-H-E-R."

"Mmmm, that's an interesting name. Here you are. You will have to have an updated card made. We are changing to a new automated checkout system, which requires special cards. Would you like for me to have a new card made for you?"

"Can I check out books today?"

"Yes, you may. Your old card is still valid. Just fill this application out." *Bet she drove home for lunch. That means I'm stuck here for a while.*

"Hey, I'm also interested in airplanes. Where might I find those books?"

I'm going to send the police after that supervisor if she doesn't show in the next ten minutes! "Let me show you where to look for those airplane books. Just follow me."

"I'm a certified pilot. In fact, I'm building an experimental airplane called a Pitts Special. It's a biplane. I'm finishing the top wing in my front room—moved the furniture into the dining room. I'm sewing the canvas onto the struts at present. By the way, what's your name?"

"Miss Teaford. Here are the airplane books."

"Say, I keep my Taylor craft hangered at the Versailles Airport. Would you like to go flying with me sometime?"

"That would be nice. Listen, I just saw my replacement arrive. I must go on my lunch break now. Hope you enjoy your books."

I grabbed my purse and made a beeline for the basement stairs and for the staff lounge. The minute I reached the bottom of the stairs I physically felt like a ton of bricks dropped on my head. Oh! How stupid can a person be! Here was a nice guy trying his best to get me to notice him! All I could think about was food! And when he asked my name, I said "Miss Teaford" of all things! I never in my life referred to myself as Miss Teaford. He must have thought I was such a prissy old librarian.

I didn't make it to the staff lounge. The next several minutes I spent berating myself for my utter lack of awareness. Then it dawned on me. I must do something to change this Mr. P-H-I-L-I-P L-E-I-B-F-A-C-H-E-R's impression of me. My subconscious must have been taking note. How would I remember that spelling otherwise?

I stumbled over my big feet trying to return up the stairs. Entering the main lobby, I glanced from side to side. No Philip. I rushed into the nonfiction room hurrying past each row hoping to catch a glimpse of a handsome young man wearing his flying coveralls (there's my sub-conscious, once again noticing details I wasn't aware it took in). I rushed into each room: the fiction room, the biography room, the reference room, and finally the Egyptian room. But he wasn't there! Oh, what had I done! I dejectedly started to return downstairs when I heard that same melodic masculine voice, "Miss Teaford?"

I turned to see those sparkling blue eyes coming toward me. "Yes?" I purred, enchanted.

"I got out to my car before I realized I hadn't asked you if I could call you."

I quickly grabbed a card and jotted down my phone number. "Yes. Call me at home." I gave him the card.

"Thanks. See ya, then."

"Yes. See you."

Jack's Story

Elizabeth was employed almost all her working life in libraries but is now retired. When we met she was working in the Greenock Public Library, Scotland, which at that time was housed in a very stately Victorian-style building adjacent to the municipal buildings in Greenock, which housed the council, the provost's office, and all the civic paraphernalia. She often had to work until 8:30 p.m. and I would spend an hour or two hanging around waiting on her. I naturally moved inside the library to benefit from the heat and of course spent hours reading as I waited.

In my time I witnessed the great and the good of the town selecting their reading material. I saw the eccentrics poring over the seedier books and the "Holy Willies" scratching out the juicier phrases so that the reader would not sully his mind by reading what they considered filth, such as James Joyce or J. P. Dunleavy. The phrases they erased pale into insignificance when compared to modern films, books, and television but at the time they were shocking.

The great benefit of having an "insider" in the library was that I was generally excused the scorching fine of two pence when returning a late book, and I was somehow spirited up the waiting list when a popular book came on the shelf. This preferential treatment may or may not have cemented our love but subsequently we married.

My wife went on to work in a medical library and in our mellowing years her ready access to the symptoms and cures of the ailments that beset the human body was another unforeseen benefit.

Whether or not the hours spent in the library affected me is arguable but I became an avid reader of the works of Robert Burns and over the last twenty-five years have spoken in many parts of the world at Burns Suppers.

Jeff's Story

I saw her for the first time yesterday, after coming to the library for a car repair manual. I have dated many girls, and they were all knockouts, but she is different. For one, she carries herself like a lady, and she's well versed as well. As I write this across from her she doesn't realize that the only reason I come here is to see if one day I can muster up the nerve to talk to her. Not so tough, right? Well I've always had a soft heart for smart, book-wise girls, and the flat shoes, the glasses, and her demeanor draw me in like a magnet. I haven't felt this way physically in so long, but the attraction isn't based on that aspect. It's more of a love for an enlightened woman.

We met in the hallway at the entrance of the library. I can always tell when a girl loves flirting with you, and she did. Her younger wit and keen intellect drove me mad inside with an unimaginable passion. I have never in my whole life known a woman so learned, so beautiful in her mind and soul. She was standing before me and through conversation I found that she and my sister were great friends. Now this has injected me with a solution of romance for her, and our next opportunity of unspoken words.

Mary's Story

[Hazel is a children's librarian who met her husband in a library when she was working in New Zealand. She sent the story of her mother, Mary Vernon, a romance written predominantly in Mary's own words with a few additions from Hazel. Mary is now seventy-seven and Hazel's father eighty-three.]

"I never thought you would come out with me, when I plucked up courage to ask you," my husband said to me the other day as we sat drinking cups of tea around the table. I replied, "Well, I never thought you would ask me!"

We were remembering a day fifty-six years ago in the lending department of a small Carnegie public library, in Haslingdon, a small town in Lancashire, in the industrial northwest of England in 1948. In many ways that day seems as clear in my mind as yesterday.

I had begun work in the library soon after leaving school a few years before and enjoyed the variety of my work as a library assistant. I had taken the first part of my library exams in the nearby city of Manchester earlier in the year and was beginning to work for the second part. Stephen had recently moved to Haslingdon from the "big smoke" of Manchester and I felt he was much too sophisticated to notice a small-town girl like myself. His parents owned one of the local butcher shops and being a keen reader he had immediately enrolled at the local library.

The first time I saw him he was standing by some bookshelves studying a book and the evening sunlight was glinting on his thick curly fair hair. Although I couldn't see his face I liked the look of his hair and broad shoulders. I quietly whispered to my friend and fellow library assistant, "Let me stamp this one's books." I wanted to see what his name was on his library ticket. I was very impressed with the book he had chosen, *Crime and Punishment* by Dostoevsky, and felt his literary tastes must be quite highbrow, not at all like my own taste for lighter fare at the time.

After that Stephen began to come into the library regularly, as he was recuperating after an appendix operation and had more time to read. When the library was quiet and my boss away in the back we began to talk more and more, and one day finally, leaning casually on the counter he asked me if I'd like to go see a film with him. Of course I said yes and six months later we were married. We have now shared a life together that has spanned three continents: emigrating to Australia (within that first year), to America some years later, and then finally back to England, seeing sights and having adventures I would never have dreamed possible as a nineteen-year-old in Haslingdon Public Library.

Margaret's Story

When I first began work in September 1950 at the Runnymede Library in Toronto, finding romance there was the furthest from my mind. As a new graduate from library school, there was a lot to learn on the job, including how to answer any and all questions.

That December, a tall gentleman wearing a brown coat and hat asked for a book by S. J. Perlman that was not on the shelf. I took a request to hold the book for him, establishing that we both liked humorous writing. He had an English accent, which caught my interest, besides being very good-looking.

I was certainly surprised and flustered one day soon after when he came to the desk and asked me out to dinner that evening. Not being very impulsive, I said no, but then qualified the refusal by saying I could go on the following evening. We went to dinner and a movie and the next week to a performance of Handel's *Messiah* at Massey Hall.

By the next summer we were engaged, and we married on June 14, 1952. I worked at the North York Library after leaving the Toronto system, then for twenty-four years in St. Thomas, Ontario. We have both been devoted library users and I still take library books to him at a nearby nursing home. We enjoyed traveling, music, and films, but the strong thread of our marriage has always been our love of books.

Margreet's Story

I am a Dutch librarian and I live in a little town in Holland. I met my husband at the library thirteen years ago, when he came in to borrow compact discs. I liked him very much. Because of that I couldn't help him because I was too scared. Eventually we married. We have two kids and are very happy together.

Bev's Story

I was a widow at the age of fifty-two who lost her husband to cancer. I had been widowed for two years and had absolutely no desire to date, never mind remarry. Working in the acquisitions department at library headquarters, the only people I ever came directly in contact with were the delivery people that I saw on a regular basis.

Being a naturally friendly person, it was always interesting to talk to these people, as it helped to break up the day. One fellow in particular was always very pleasant and very professional, and we would chat for a few minutes each week when he came in. He was the sales rep for the company that supplied us with the magazines and paperbacks that we received weekly as a standing order. I had continued to wear my wedding rings, so he assumed that I was married until we had a conversation around Christmas that left him wondering about my status. He talked to the rep that used to come in before he started and of course was informed that I was a widow, whereupon he asked me out for dinner.

When this invitation came so unexpectedly, I was at a bit of a loss, so put him off with an excuse about a sick mother. When he came the following week he asked me once again to go out for dinner, but I declined the invitation, saying instead that I would meet him at the local shopping center in the Food Fair area, which is a very public place, the following Saturday. He was a bit taken aback, but did agree. (After all, he could have been a serial rapist for all I knew.)

The following Saturday we had a coffee and then went for a walk in the park. It was a beautiful June day and I gave him the third degree. He was very forthcoming, and when I asked him what happened with his previous marriage and he said he didn't really know, but that his ex-wife had been carrying on with another man for a year unbeknownst to him and his daughters, I told him that he mustn't have been paying attention. The phrase "paying attention" is now a private joke between the two of us.

In our conversation in the park I quizzed him on the relationship between him and his mother and daughters. I gathered that they saw a lot of each other, so I determined that if they liked him, he probably was a pretty nice guy. Over the next few months I was able to see the interaction between them, so I knew everything was okay in that department.

On one of our first dates we went to a retirement party for one of his coworkers. I was taken aside by a fellow who had worked with him for years and was basically told not to fool with the poor guy's emotions, as he had been going through a very bad time. I thought that was rather sweet, actually, and gave me a further indication that he was a very well-liked fellow.

As the months progressed we saw a lot of each other, and we both knew we had something rather special. Just before New Year's Day he proposed to me (on his knees, no less), and when I said yes, it took three Scotches to settle him down.

We have just celebrated our fifth wedding anniversary, and are still in love and still having fun.

Notes

1. www.nytimes.com/2004/07/11/fashion/weddings/11VOWS.html.
2. All names in this story are pseudonyms.
3. Pseudonym.

CHAPTER EIGHT

~

Bookmobile Romance

Carol's Story

I met my second husband in 1985 or so, when I was asked to do a workshop on bookmobiles for the state of South Carolina. I was head of the outreach department at my library and had published a couple of articles on bookmobiles, but since there was almost no other literature on bookmobiles at the time, that made me as close to an expert as they could get, I guess.

Libby Law at the South Carolina State Library called me about doing the workshop. I said I'd love to but I couldn't talk about the mechanical aspect of bookmobiles. She said, "No problem. We have a great guy here in South Carolina who fixes bookmobiles for the whole state and he's going to do the mechanics part." I was delighted.

At the workshop I was introduced to Russ Topping, the aforesaid mechanic. I had set up the workshop so that we would talk for a few minutes about various aspects of each topic (selecting a vendor, collection development, PR, deciding where to stop, or whatever) and then let the attendees discuss topics among themselves, after which we would hear what they had found out.

We did it that way because I long ago observed that you usually learn more from your peers at conferences than from the "expert" speakers. But the result was that Russ and I had nothing to do but talk to each other for the discussion part of each hour, so we got to know each other. At the time we were both married to other people, and the talk was strictly about libraries, but I have always liked guys who can do things, so I liked him a lot.

After that, several other libraries asked us to do workshops, including two for Georgia and one for the state of Louisiana, so we got to know each other better. Meanwhile, two things happened. First, Russ began manufacturing bookmobiles which—typical for him—were revolutionary. For instance, they had no generators. (At the time most bookmobiles had gas generators and they were the plague of bookmobile librarians' lives.) Second, my library decided to buy a new bookmobile, so naturally I included Russ among the vendors asked to bid. I was very pleased when Russ got the bid because I knew he was open to new ideas, so we began having regular telephone talks about the detailed specifications.

Meanwhile, both of our respective spouses had initiated divorces (nothing to do with the relationship between Russ and me, which was strictly business up to then). Naturally, we began talking about that, too. We also met at the Ohio conference and became closer.

These were economic hard times—small businesses were shutting down all over. Between that and the financial disaster of his divorce, Russ had to shut his formerly thriving shop in South Carolina, so he brought my library's partly finished new tractor-trailer bookmobile to Gainesville, Florida, where I live, to finish it. He rented a shop and an apartment here.

By that point we were falling in love. However, we knew that marrying the builder of my new bookmobile would look like a conflict of interest, so we held off involvement until well after the bookmobile was completed and delivered in August 1987. At the time it was the most innovative bookmobile in the country and seventeen years later it is still going strong and still innovative (because standard bookmobiles have really not changed all that much).

We finally got married in November 1998 and lived happily ever after until Russ died in February 2002. We set up a bookmobile consulting firm (though I kept my library job too) and spent a lot of time speaking at conferences, writing on bookmobiles, and doing workshops. We traveled all over and had a great time. I always told audiences that marrying Russ showed that some librarians will do *anything* for a good bookmobile. That always got a laugh, but in fact, he was wonderful.

He was so loving that he made me feel like a queen. He was a great cook, so when I'd come home from the library in the evening, dinner was ready. He also brought me breakfast in bed every morning for years. Besides that bonus, he could build or repair absolutely anything. In the fourteen years we were married I never had to call a painter, electrician, plumber, carpenter, auto mechanic, HVAC repairer, or any other mechanical tradespeople. Our house was full of little conveniences he built for me, many of which I still have. For instance, when we bought our house it had three outside faucets. When I sold the house after his death it had eight. The whole house was like that. Needless to say, I was spoiled rotten! Romance *and* mechanical genius—what else could a woman want? All my friends envied me.

I miss him every day and according to the e-mail I get, a lot of book-mobile librarians, who used to rely on him for advice, miss him too. He loved librarians and loved helping them—I was just the lucky one who got to marry him.

I can certainly recommend library romance to everybody.

Keli's Story

My boyfriend and I met at the Topeka and Shawnee County Public Library in Topeka, Kansas, in 2000. He worked in the bookmobile department while I was an adult services paraprofessional. I had already worked there for about two years and he was new when we met on a staff development day. We were just friends until near the end of 2002 when we fell in love. He moved with me to Florida in January 2003 so that I could attend graduate school for library and information science at the University of South Florida. We are still doing great together and shall soon be moving from Tampa to Jacksonville, Florida, where I shall begin my professional career at Jacksonville Public Library as a reference librarian.

Susan's Story[1]

Susan moved to Winnipeg, Manitoba, in the late 1970s to be with her widowed mother. In 1978, her brother invited her to visit him in Fort

McMurray, in northern Alberta. A week later she was hired as a library clerk by the local public library.

Fort McMurray was a boom town because of its vast, government-sponsored oil projects. Susan was working six days a week, including Thursday evenings, when the oil workers would come in to read the newspapers and magazines. It was a very friendly atmosphere, although sometimes too friendly—such as the time "Big Al" came in and asked for a date. A short but nightmarish relationship followed, leaving Susan with a rule that in the future, her personal address wouldn't be given out to prospective dates.

So when Bruce asked to take her out, Susan arranged for him to pick her up at the library. When he insisted he was divorced she asked him to bring his papers to prove it—which he did. They began dating regularly, meeting at the library, until Susan felt, in this small town, she could safely divulge where she lived. It turned out they were both residents of the same apartment building.

They married. Susan was in charge of the library's bookmobile service for the next ten years. She couldn't have done it without Bruce, she affirms. He designed, created, tweaked, and fixed things for her for free—not just when she ran the bookmobile, but throughout their life together.

Bruce and Susan had never talked about having pets, although she was very fond of animals. Once she parked the bookmobile in the dead of winter in the local college parking lot. The key challenge in those temperatures was to get the big diesel engine running. Susan's normal pattern was to rush to the front door, get the engine warm, and go. One day for some reason she stopped at the desk on the way, and heard a cat mewing. She discovered the cat under the hood, and brought it into the library.

The cat turned out to be pregnant. It miscarried six kittens on their bed. They put her in the bathtub for safety overnight, and Susan begged her supervisor the following morning for time to take the cat to the vet. The cat became Scampers the bookmobile cat, and lived with Susan and Bruce for eighteen years.

On Tuesday evenings, she took the bookmobile to the oil workers' camps. It was a very popular service, although one visitor (one of the many lonely men working there) suggested another service the library could provide from the bookmobile. Susan waved her hand in front of him and said, "Look, I'm engaged to be married," to which the oilman answered, "I ain't looking for commitment."

Bookmobiles all over the world suffer from the same mechanical problems, Susan claims. Bruce, who had become an aficionado of the big diesel beasts, would chase bookmobiles they spotted on vacation and engage the drivers in conversation about the universal problems of their furnaces and air conditioners.

Bruce was a huge supporter of Susan and her work. When the Friends of the Library bought a custom-built diesel rig, Susan had to go to air rig school to get her air brake license. She was the only woman in the class. The other students were angry that a woman was taking a "man's job." When they discovered she was "the library lady," they befriended her. Susan was terrified of failing the class, but Bruce taught her the inner workings of the engine so that she could pass the exam. She took copious verbatim notes over the month-long course, and Bruce would patiently explain them to her.

The college had eighteen-wheelers to learn on. At only five feet tall, Susan needed a ladder to get into the cab. The first step up was at shoulder height. Driving was terrifying. But on Sundays, Bruce would take her to the parking lot and painstakingly teach her how to back up. Susan passed the course with high marks.

By the late 1980s the bookmobile's circulation figures were matching those of the main library. A small van had been added to provide homebound service to seniors. Bruce continued to offer practical and moral support, and Susan was nominated Citizen of the Day on a Canadian Broadcasting Corporation (CBC) radio show by grateful patrons. In the peak of the severe winters she continued to feel scared driving out to the camps on a very dangerous road, where cooped-up oil workers drove like maniacs. Bruce's advice was to look at the size of the rig she was driving: "It's your road—own it."

By the time Susan and Bruce left Fort McMurray in 1993, the bookmobile service had been shut down, a victim of the far-reaching government cutbacks of that period. They moved to Nanaimo on Vancouver Island, and Susan commuted by ferry to Gabriola Island, where she was made branch head of the regional library system. Bruce had been a carpenter by trade, and built schools and a seniors' complex on First Nations land. When at one point a shelf fell down in the library, he came straight away to fix it back in place. He called all his handyman activities for the library his volunteer work.

When Bruce died in 2003, Susan felt she had to resign. She saw him in every nook and cranny in the library. After twenty-three years of sharing her library career and so much more with Bruce it was all so different without him, and she suddenly found that libraries weren't a passion for her any more.

Recently Susan began attending university. She believes she is still relying on Bruce's strength and everlasting love to keep her going down new roads. He was her biggest advocate. He used to read westerns when he first came to the library. But over the years he became a military history buff. He told her, "When you open the door to your mind, you open the door to your heart."

Note

1. Telephone interview with the editor, October 18, 2004.

CHAPTER NINE

~

The Romance of Special Libraries

A Marriage Made in Heaven—
John J. Heney

Research is in my blood. It's found me lurking among the stacks in archives and libraries from Dawson City to Dublin, from Washington to Warsaw, in all manner of assignments linked to work in journalism, political science, and international affairs. Truly a passion, it also led to romance, and a fairy-tale wedding.

In 1980, at the age of twenty-four, I had been hired in Ottawa as the first analyst in telecommunications regulation at Bell-Northern Research (BNR), an outfit long since swallowed up by its larger parent, Nortel. Linked to information and data of all kinds, it was no surprise that my office was attached to BNR's corporate library—the Technical Information Centre (TIC).

What I didn't know was that my boss's boss was also the boss of the boss of my future wife, a woman who would agree to my marriage proposal within seventeen days of our first meeting, on our second date.

Kathy Davidson was at work at the TIC's Montreal branch. When she joined TIC staff from other locations for a conference in Ottawa, I was on the roster of speakers. You can still see the two of us in a photograph, within hours of meeting. We're standing alone together, off in a corner of the garden, absorbed in each other's company while, nearby, everyone else enjoys the hospitality that ensued at the home of a staff member.

Others must have noticed too. When Kathy left, I thought my good-bye, though sincere, had not been too obvious. But my coffee and dessert were suddenly removed from my hands as I was purposely and inexplicably whisked away by onlookers—through the garden, through the house, and into the car with Kathy. Surely, I was told, our hostess's husband, who was taking her to the bus terminal for her trip back to Montreal, would appreciate the company, seeing how Kathy had refused the entreaties of our mutual director that she could, by all means, stay the night.

I dutifully returned with her chauffeur to the party, not discovering until later how bets had been taken as to whether I would return or come to my senses about the obvious. What amateur cupids!—if there ever was a double meaning.

They were the ones in for a surprise. In the days that followed, Kathy and I communicated by corporate phone line, interoffice mail, and via the very rudimentary e-mail of the early 1980s. Having already planned a weekend in Montreal before we met, I took her out to dinner there within days, and she accepted an invitation to see me in Ottawa. It was then, in Ottawa, that I proposed.

Yes, she agreed on the spot. Yes, our colleagues and family were surprised.

It gets better.

Ever a bird dog, hunting down information, I had latched on to that treasure hunt of treasure hunts called genealogy. Back in 1976, not content just to find out that my great-great-grandfather, the Irish-born Ottawa merchant and politician named John Heney, had been granted a papal knighthood in 1896, I'd set out to discover the details.

One result was my ensuing friendship with Monsignor Renato Martino, First Secretary of the Vatican diplomatic delegation to Canada—along with a lighthearted gentlemen's agreement. Should he ever be elevated in the Church, I would attend the ceremony. He—if ever the occasion arose—would officiate at my wedding.

Just seven months before meeting Kathy, I found myself being escorted by the Swiss Guard through the marble hallways of the Vatican. I was on my way to the private apartment of Pope John Paul II to meet the pontiff himself, there a guest for the ordination of my friend.

The newly appointed archbishop, no less, would become the Holy See's diplomatic delegate to Southeast Asia.

Now back in Ottawa, I looked at the calendar with my bride-to-be. I phoned with my news to Bangkok, much to the joy of the man on the other end of the line. Kathy and I would wait out the rigorous part-time studies for my master's in international affairs. We would be married on Saturday, July 9, 1983—two years to the very day we had first met.

The congregation assembled before us on our wedding day at St. Joseph's Church in Ottawa was in for more than the surprise of witnessing Archbishop Martino officiate. With the exchange of the rings completed, our friend surprised us all with two gifts from the Pope himself—a telegram of blessings to us and our families, and a beautiful white rosary for Kathy.

Renato explained it all in the limousine on the way to the reception, chuckling how, as he sat between us, he ought not to be the one to put asunder the union he'd only just completed. That very morning, he had addressed officials among Canada's bishops about the pending papal tour scheduled to take place in Canada the next year. In preparation, he had not traveled to us through Vancouver as we'd thought, but rather around the world the other way, stopping for a breakfast meeting with the Pope.

"John's getting married?" asked the Pope.

And married John and Kathy still are.

Moral: Do your research. Be polite, but always dare to ask questions. And be courteous to those librarians. They may have what you need, or know who does. And maybe . . . just maybe . . . one may kiss you. Right between the stacks.

Erda's[1] Story

I met my husband at the place where I was the librarian, and he, an astronomer. We were located at two thousand four hundred meters altitude, and could enjoy the fabulous southern sky. He would go to the library and borrow some books, which I noticed he would return sooner than other scientists! Since my schedule was to work at the mountain every two weeks, it was a different setting for a romance. Instead of the city, we had the mountains, and the most glorious sunsets. He proposed one evening, when the sun was about to disappear in the horizon, and together we saw the rare green flash.

We are happy after twenty years of marriage.

Melissa's Story

I met my husband while I was working as a librarian in his pharmaceutical company. The company relocated the library space to one of the lab buildings, but due to a shortage of available cubes, the library ended up housing two of the scientists along with the books, the journals, and me. One was my future husband, Tim.

Being the only nonscientist in the building was interesting, but Tim was in the small group who welcomed me wholeheartedly, especially since we shared a small space together. I ended up eating lunch with him and two other scientists every day. One of my jobs was to acquire research articles and deliver them. He always had a lot of requests, but would always apologize or offer to get them himself if I was too busy. I also was in charge of archiving the lab notebooks, something the scientists always gave me fits about, but Tim always saw my side of things and was very nice and made sure that I knew that what I did was appreciated. We never did anything outside of work, though, and we never thought we were anything more than friends.

Then, one fateful day in January 2002, I got laid off. I managed to tell almost everyone I was leaving but forgot to tell Tim. I was escorted out of the building (as is protocol—very humiliating) but later realized I had left my cell phone at my desk. I wasn't sure when I'd be let back in to clean out my desk, so I snuck around the back of the building and knocked on Tim's window, since he was by the door. He didn't realize I had been laid off so he made some snide remark about getting locked out. I breezed by him, yelling that I didn't want to hear it and that I no longer had a job. When I came back through his area, he was standing in the same spot and he was crying. I felt terrible. He apologized for my losing my job, told me to call him if I ever needed anything, and asked me out to dinner. We've been together ever since.

Tim has become a major library supporter and helped me find the perfect job. He said he never knew that being married to a librarian could be so interesting. His first love note to me detailed the story of the librarian and the scientist: the perfect match.

Hilary's[2] Story

I was married for thirty-one years to a man who was a prominent special librarian for the last seventeen years of his life. He died some time ago, a much loved and respected leader of the library. The institution decided to soldier on without replacing him for twelve months—this was seen as a healing time for those who had become a very strong team, like a family. During those twelve months, the library committee appointed another subject specialist to assist with the day-to-day issues that could arise.

This scientist was new to the faculty, and only known to me by reputation. As it happened, he and I became very good friends, a friendship which grew as he continued to keep me up to date on the goings and comings in the library, etc. As well, he introduced me to a love of his subject and we would discuss this for quite some time, often being the only two left after an event or gathering.

Eventually, he decided that perhaps we could have a meal together and from there we grew closer, were engaged, and married a little over two years ago. He has a very large library at home, spread over two studies, as well as stored books in the built-in wardrobes and linen press—something that I had to gently alter before I could move in! He also has a library at his college office that spreads onto the floor and under and over his desk, not to mention the shelves he has also "borrowed" from another lecturer. His second study at home, also filled with books, is now my study, but I have had to put my books in front of his in order to accommodate my collection. Fortunately, his books in my library are those that are not used as much by him.

At our wedding reception I read a poem to him that suggested that I thought he might have married me in order to have someone catalog all his books, and, foolishly, I promised to do so!

I have continued to love and share the study of my husband's field, and as a consequence my library has grown also! He is still on the library committee, so I still feel involved and aware of that library's comings and goings, and one of the joys which we share will always be the love of books and reading.

Ben and Toni's Story

Ben:
I met Toni on my first day of my new job. I was halfway through the "grand tour" when I was taken into the library and introduced to Toni. My first day at work was a blur—I was introduced to a hundred and eighty or so people and I could only remember one with any detail: the friendly girl in the library with a very pretty face. Over the next year or so we struck up a friendship. I was involved with someone else at the time, and the worse the relationship with my ex got, the better the relationship with Toni became. Soon after, I was single again and as I was in the IT department, Toni was resorting to breaking her computer on purpose to keep me around. It seemed like I spent most of my time hanging around the library—either fixing mysterious problems or chatting to Toni. I used to buy her chocolate bars, but I had to buy everybody one so that Toni would think I was nice but not too keen—trying to play it cool, so to speak. But I don't think anyone was fooled.

I gave the game away, as it was costing me a packet, and asked her out on a date. We both had a wonderful time and have been inseparable ever since. We were married on the December 8, 2003, in Las Vegas.

It is hard enough picking just one piece of music which defines your relationship with a friend, let alone the love of your life. There are just so many great songs that mean a lot to me, but if I had to choose one it would be "From Me to You" by the Beatles. The first verse is perfect for us because we would do anything for each other.

Toni:
I met the love of my life in a library.

After years of complaining to my mum that my knight in shining armor must be coming on a donkey and riding up a steep hill because he was taking so long, my complaints vanished on the day that I met my Ben. I was working as a library assistant in a law firm's private library and met Ben on his first day at work. Ben was being shown around the library and all I remember on that day was how tall Ben was, his smile, and that everything seemed so much brighter . . . like a light was shining out of him. I also thought, "The knight and donkey have arrived!"

Ben and I were friends from the very second we met. I looked forward to seeing him every day and we had so much in common. Ben would visit the library and we would sit and talk on our lunch break amongst the books.

My friendship turned to love when I was going on vacation and realized I wouldn't be seeing Ben for over six weeks. I knew then that I loved him and would miss him terribly and felt sad that I couldn't tell him that. When I came back to work after my holiday, Ben looked so happy to see me and the friendship sparkle we always had in our eyes started looking to me like a love sparkle. I felt very excited. That's when I started breaking our computers. Ben worked in the IT department and was in charge of fixing our computers and making sure they ran smoothly. Because Ben always came down to our library to fix problems, I realized this was a good way of seeing him more often, so I started deleting documents, pulling power cables out of the computers, and acting like a helpless twit. It worked. (Having big boobs also didn't hurt.)

One day, I caught Ben looking at me in a way that made me blush when I was shelving books. I looked up and saw him staring and instead of him looking away because he'd been caught, he held his stare and smiled. That's when I knew he liked me too.

Ben asked me on our first date at the library. It was romantic and I will never forget it. My heart felt like it was going to jump out of my body and lie on the floor. It was the start of many dates and then living together, then my leaving to work in another library because people started to find out we were together and whispered and stared whenever we were together.

Ben and I are married now. We believe that marriage is a private and meaningful event that should just be meant for each other, so we saved our money and got married in Las Vegas. Our wedding song was "He Needs Me" by Shelley Duvall from the movie *Punch Drunk Love*. The photographer and minister both commented that in all the marriages they had seen, nobody had ever used that song. We love being original!

It was the best trip we have ever had together so far. We are each other's best friend and I don't know what I would ever do without him.

Lebogang's Story

He is tall and light in complexion, with a bald patch and a smile to die for. I've seen him around the law library a few times. I thought to myself wow!—I'd love to know this guy better, but he's so quiet and very soft-spoken, so much so that I thought talking to him would be a bother. Nevertheless, he would take a little piece of me with him every time he walked past. He would come past and greet me, then disappear in a short while. Just the other day, he came over and asked a few of the lousiest questions over and over. He walked away, and then later came back again to ask me to show him one of the *Acts* on the shelf. As I was walking beside him, I could feel my knees going weak. As he got closer to look into the *Act* with me, the smell of his perfume was incredibly nice. I must have gone mad at that moment because I found myself asking him a question: "How does it feel like to be the most handsome guy on the floor at this moment?"

"Excuse me?" he asked. I repeated the question. Silence followed. I was beginning to feel really stupid because I looked at him and thought he felt offended. I walked away, silently hoping the ground would open up and swallow me. I realized that I gave the poor guy the shock of his life. A few minutes later, when he had caught his breath, he came back and we exchanged numbers.

We had a date the following day and it was the happiest day of my life when we finally talked things through. I found out that I was the only reason he came into the law library. I also found out that he is Sudanese, unmarried, unattached, thirty-four years old with a good sense of humor. I'm twenty-nine years old (soon to be thirty). Despite the fact that we have different religions—he's Islamic and I'm a Christian—we had the most incredible connection I've ever had with anyone before. We started going out on June 10, 2004, and I still think he's the most wonderful guy I've ever met and he still makes me laugh the same way. I never see him in the library anymore. He told me that the only reason why he always came to the library was to try and strike up a conversation with me. Now that he can see me anytime outside the library, he feels no need to come over there anymore.

Anna's[3] Story

Our romance is probably one in a million. A prison library is not so unusual you would think, until you know that my husband was an inmate and I worked part time in the library. Any personal contact between inmates and staff is forbidden and I have to say that although there was an attraction between us, nothing unprofessional happened while I was working at the prison. My husband was detailed to be a library orderly and we met on his first day. It was my job to explain his duties and teach him the computer skills necessary to circulate books. Though it was unknown to me, my husband told me afterward that it was love at first sight for him, although he had always dismissed this saying as rubbish! It was obvious from the start that we had an affinity toward each other. Having similar personalities, we found that working together was easy and we anticipated each other. This is very useful when you get a group of twenty men in the library at the same time all wanting immediate attention. We thoroughly enjoyed each other's company, and my husband has the unique quality of making me laugh at the most inopportune moments. My feelings for him grew rapidly as I tried to keep myself in check, knowing that I could not show how I felt. He also was very professional. However, we always tried to work together as often as possible.

My husband worked in the library for three months, after which he was released back into society. Working in the library was not the same after he left and I missed him terribly. Before he left I was given his cell phone number with the invitation to phone him if I so wished (although contacting former inmates was not allowed by the prison ser-vice). Of course I phoned him and we met in a town between where we both lived. We just never looked back from there, and within three weeks we were living together. As soon as we were living together I left the prison library and am now employed at another library. We have been married for sixteen months and are blissfully happy, living in our happy home with our mad dog and budgie.

Notes

1. Pseudonym.
2. Pseudonym.
3. Pseudonym.

CHAPTER TEN

Intralibrary Romance

William's Story

I met the most amazing woman at my library. Our relationship started out as a "just friends" kind of thing: two people going out and having a little fun with the coworkers. But the more time she and I spent together, the more we realized we weren't dating, we were just steadily becoming partners who cared about each other. Sure, we have had some ups and downs. Who doesn't? And maybe she reads romance novels and I prefer biographies, but we have worked things out. Our love of sushi and small chirping animals—and even our differences—has drawn us closer.

We only worked together for six months and she was transferred out, which we think was because someone complained about our romance (and maybe we got into a little hanky-panky in the library once or twice, but that's another story). We continued to see each other. She supported me through the death of my mother. I have grown close to her family. We were tested, and yet we came through it stronger than ever. I don't see her as a girlfriend anymore. I don't see her as a friend, either. She has turned into a partner in the truest sense of companionship: a companion, loyal, unpredictable, the person I call first to tell about my day, someone I care enough about to be involved in her life and world, and whom I can't envision not being a part of my life, that person who at the end of the day is the perfect cuddling buddy to rest with and groom each other and fall asleep. We both continue to work in the library system and enjoy being library nerds together.

Christine's Story

We met when we were both working in lowly clerical positions at the Halifax Memorial Library (as it was then called) in Nova Scotia. He was seventeen, working full time for a year between high school and university. I was nineteen, working part time while doing my bachelor's degree. We discovered a shared sense of humor while sorting the circulation slips (they were paper and sorted by hand in those days), shelf-reading, and shelving book trucks. Our first date was on a Friday the thirteenth in January.

We became an item, and continued to be seriously involved while I was off at library school in Vancouver (there was no local library school then) and he was at McGill University in Montreal. We even got engaged at a tender age. But it was not to be . . . yet.

We lived on different continents, pursued studies and careers, kept in and out of touch, even got briefly involved again a couple of times over the years, and finally we both ended up back in the Maritimes. We started seeing each other again. On another January Friday the thirteenth, exactly twenty-two years since our first date, we got engaged for the second time. Now we have been happily married for fifteen years and counting. Better late than never!

Jennifer's Story

My husband Chris and I have both worked in the Phoenix Public Library for years. He works in the periodicals department and I work in information services.

For five years we never spoke to each other: although our departments are on the same floor, our paths rarely crossed. I was engaged to someone and he was dating someone else, and both were long-term relationships. Both of those relationships ended within months of each other, unbeknownst to us. In an effort to get me out and circulating, another coworker asked me to go to a bar to see the band of "that guy from periodicals" play. I consulted my horoscope for that day and it said, "You'll meet your soul mate at a social gathering," so I went.

A life-changing moment, for sure: that shy guy from periodicals was the lead singer/guitar player and he had such an amazing stage presence. I was dumbstruck. I sent him an e-mail telling him how much I enjoyed his band The Cartwheels and to let me know when they played again. He e-mailed back a wonderful story about band life versus library life. I was a struggling writer then (now I write romantic comedy for Harlequin), so I appreciated his witty e-mail. Our friendship bloomed. He gave me a tape with a wonderful song called "Butterflies" on it.

I came to find out six months later, when we began dating, that he had had a crush on me for years and had written the song for me one day when he had said something that made me laugh. We were married the following year and now have two sons, who are the lights of our lives and are frequently referred to as the "library babies" by our coworkers.

We both still work at Phoenix Public. He works full time and I work part time, and we arrange our schedules around each other's so that one of us is always with our kids. I believe it was fate that we found each other at Phoenix Public Library.

Leah's Story

I began work at the Durango Public Library in October 2000. In September 2002, the library hired Steve. He was one of only three men working there, and was quite single. You know how it is in a workplace full of ladies: humorous—but very false—rumors began to circulate about Steve and several other women working there. Our romance began in March 2003, and we tried very hard to keep things quiet, as the rumors were a nuisance, and we weren't sure what others (especially our superiors) would think.

After about a month, there were so many new rumors that we decided to share the news of our relationship, and most people were happy for us. Unfortunately, as the library is open seven days a week, Steve and I were working opposite schedules, and it wasn't until after we were engaged more than a year later that our schedules fell into sync. We are scheduled to be married in September 2004.

Although we both have plenty of library experience, neither of us is your "typical" librarian. We are outdoor addicts, hikers, bikers, canyon explorers. We are also peace and environmental activists who travel regularly to see "hippie" jam bands like Phish and String Cheese Incident. Needless to say, our wedding will be anything but traditional, and we are inviting the whole library staff. More good news: the City of Durango has given our library permission to close early that day so everyone can attend!

John's Story

I began my library career as a college student in 1969. Arthur Curley, who was then director of the Montclair Public Library in New Jersey, hired me for a neighborhood outreach project. Our assignment involved a bookmobile which made the rounds of parks and school yards during the summer months. We had paperbacks available for borrowing, the ability to register folks (mostly children) for library cards, and often a storyteller on board.

The following year, I joined the staff full time. Twelve years later, in 1982, Mary Lou came to Montclair, first as head of cataloging, then as head of reference. The library underwent several major changes in organizational structure during this time. When Mary Lou assumed a new position as head of adult services, my department came under that umbrella and she became my supervisor.

Mary Lou and I continued working together, though in different parts of the building, and remained on good terms. At the time, we had no interaction outside the library and were still getting to know one another. Then in 1989, we came up with an idea for an adult school course. We called it "Page to Screen." Students were asked to read a novel or short story prior to each class. As a group, we'd screen a film based on the book, then discuss the finer points of each cinematic adaptation over coffee and cake.

It was through the experience of teaching this course that Mary Lou and I really got to know one another. As I am fond of telling people when they ask about our story, "That's when all the trouble started." We'd meet weekends at my parents' house to screen 16 mm films we were considering for the class. I remember one night in particular when we viewed a film based on D. H. Lawrence's *Sons and Lovers*. There was a rather steamy love scene in the film which seemed to affect us both in unexpected ways!

I remember, too, our first dinner date at a local Mexican restaurant.

A group of strolling musicians serenaded us with "Besame Mucho," which instantly became our song. We felt a bit awkward about our relationship in the early days because we both dislike gossip and hoped to avoid it. Eventually, Mary Lou felt compelled to "confess" to her supervisor, a woman she respected and considered a trusted friend.

Finally, in February of 2000, we became engaged and set the date for December 2, calling ours "the last great wedding of the century." The wedding itself was a simple affair but lots of fun. We hired a very old hotel, the Marlboro Inn, as the site for our reception. The guests were limited to family and a few of our closest friends.

The musicians were also old friends. They knew all the old standards and agreed to play "Besame Mucho" for us, but the band leader came up with another chestnut, a number called "Heaven Can Wait." He decided that should be our wedding song, so we agreed there could be two.

We're still happily married, almost four years later: a love story that began in the stacks and has had a most happy ending.

Tasneem's Story

Dennis was working as a part-time library technician at the Anaheim Public Library. I was Tasneem Ghazali at the time and had just completed my master's degree in library and information science at age forty-two. I was hired as the young adult librarian, and I was definitely *not* looking for a husband! I'd just divorced in 1995, was raising my two daughters alone, and was very cautious about dating.

From talking with Dennis while on desk, I knew that he was a musician and that he enjoyed music of all types. I wanted to go to the Orange County Irish Fair in October 1999 to see a favorite local Irish group, the Fenians. So I asked Dennis if he'd like to go with me, and he said yes.

We hit it off, finding many common interests (museums, movies, music, reading, bookstores, etc.), along with the fact that we both came to library work late in life. We began seeing each other whenever possible, but I was cautious about introducing him to my daughters until I was sure. Coworkers at Anaheim were kept in the dark, as we were discreet about our dating for several months.

Dennis had worked in the retail world, managing Florsheim shoe stores for more than fifteen years. I had worked for eleven years in hospitals, as a lab technician and in training hospital personnel about medical malpractice defense. I'd also had ten years off work while my children were small, and during that time I volunteered and developed extensive contacts with schools and libraries in the community. Soon after we began seeing each other, Dennis quit his part-time job at Anaheim and accepted a full-time job in the El Camino College Music Library in Torrance.

Dennis and I married on May 11, 2000, and are thrilled that we did! We have four kids between us. We feel very fortunate and lucky to have found each other, and we are thoroughly enjoying all our kids as they grow up.

Julie's Story

My husband and I met through working for Colchester, Essex Library in the UK back in 1995. We were by no means the only library romance: there were two married couples working there. After us there was one more wedding, and another couple moved in together. It became a bit of a running joke when positions came up, about the library matchmaking service.

Mark was a library assistant (then aged twenty-two) who had been there about a year and I was a Saturday assistant (aged sixteen) who had just started. He was my first boyfriend and I was his first girlfriend. I had only gone in to get some books for my high school courses; I came out with a job and ultimately a husband. It set me up for life.

I thought he was lovely the first moment I saw him. The only thing was, the first time I spoke to him he was having a bad day and snapped at me. We dallied about for a year, just fancying each other until a friend of mine threatened that if I didn't ask him out, she would do it for me (she would have)! I asked him out on the back stairs, though I'm not aware that anyone heard us. But, as you know, gossip in libraries travels amazingly fast and by the time we had left the stairwell everyone knew!

Most people were fine with the idea, apart from one manager who attempted to take disciplinary action on numerous occasions, though she never had good reason. She didn't get very far though as the "big boss" was married to one of the librarians. When they retired, however, things turned quite nasty for me. That manager made it clear that I should be the one to go, as I was the junior member of staff. I put up with it for nearly three years, and then I left a few months before our wedding in 1999. As soon as we were engaged, Mark was promoted to senior library assistant. It was very old-fashioned: they wanted to see you married, or engaged with your own home, before any promotions.

In 2001 Mark was promoted to manager at another branch, and it became okay for me to return to work at the central library, which I did for nearly two years as library assistant, then enquiry officer. Then we decided to move closer to Mark's branch.

We both have very fond memories of our time at the city library and how we met. Many of our memories of courting are of events that happened in the library, like the time when I made him laugh so much he dropped his sandwich. That was the moment when I knew I loved him and it was before we were going out!

Leah's Story

In 1995 I began work at Wangaratta Library in Victoria, Australia, and became firm friends with Brendan, a coworker. Not being from Wangaratta, I had visited the town on a couple of occasions for a night out with friends and remembered seeing Brendan at one of the town's night spots, though we hadn't spoken. After approximately twelve months, we realized we had something more than a friendship happening. We tried to hide our romance from other coworkers at first, but they soon guessed.

Eventually, we bought a house and in 2001, we married. We are now expecting our first baby. We still work together to a certain degree, Brendan in the branch and I in headquarters. There are only a couple of doors between us.

Leslie's Story

My husband, Alan, and I met in the appropriately named Love Library at the University of Nebraska–Lincoln, in November of 1972. Initially he and I were coworkers in the library. We were both reference librarians. We started out as friends and colleagues but after he resigned to return to school to earn an MBA, we began dating. In May 1978, we were married and still are today. We don't have a song but any song from that time period brings back many fond memories—even the Nebraska fight song.

I am still a librarian (at the University of Colorado at Colorado Springs—UCCS) but Alan, a "fallen away" librarian, works in management for the federal government.

The UCCS library has had several requests from students and alumni to use it to have their wedding. So far the red tape of insurance and parking has prevented this. But I am hoping one day it will happen.

Ed's Story

As a newly hired bibliographer at a large university library, I quickly got to know my colleagues in the acquisitions department, and I soon met the folks working in the adjoining cataloging department. Among the many talented people working there was an attractive redhead who was an expediter, who tried to move along the cataloging backlog then plaguing the technical services division.

The backlog was stored in the library basement along with unprocessed material from the university's special collections. I wanted to see the magnitude of the problem, and the redhead offered to show me. The uncataloged books were just that: a bunch of books. My interest was directed, however, to the items headed to special collections. The most unusual item was actor Roddy McDowell's makeup kit, an object which inspired much laughter and much delight.

My next encounter with the redhead occurred when I needed a babysitter. Friends with children were visiting, and I desperately needed a sitter so my two friends, my date, and I could go out for an evening. I mentioned my plight to a group of unattached colleagues at the library, but only the redhead offered to babysit.

The evening ended early. I dropped off my date and went to fetch the babysitter to take her home. But we stayed up until three in the morning, chatting, drinking wine, and becoming completely smitten with one another. We announced our engagement four months later.

Alice's Story

In the 1970s I was working at the National Library of Canada. The National Archives was in the same building and the staff often took courses together. While on a French course, I met a very handsome, charming archivist and we were very strongly drawn to each other. We were both married with children and tried very hard to resist the attraction but the pull was too strong and we finally succumbed.

We have been together now for twenty-four years, have a wonderful twenty-year-old daughter, and a blended family of children and grandchildren. They all get along very well, as do many of our friends who have remained supportive of us.

My husband has been retired for several years and I have changed careers. While still working together we enjoyed attending many learned society conferences across Canada and welcomed any opportunity to travel and take courses together.

We are both voracious readers and when I read stories about romance, love, attraction, and all types of relationships, I realize that my true life story can rival any of those.

Mark's Story

After returning home from a five-year stay in the United States (I'm a graduate of Amherst College in Massachusetts), I landed a job at the University of Cape Town Library. There I met my wife Shanaaz, who had been working there for a year. We started dating almost immediately and were engaged about two years later in June 1995. During the courting phase of our relationship, we were often caught kissing between the stacks.

Nancy's Story

I met the love of my life at the Providence Public Library in Providence, Rhode Island. I work as a manager in the administrative offices and he came in as a temp in the office. We found that we had much in common and became good friends. Before he left we had a little falling out. I was devastated. He didn't know it at the time, but I had already thought of him as the man I was supposed to spend the rest of my life with. And according to the romance novels I read, he was supposed to realize that and proclaim his love for me too!

A short time after he left, he sent me a wonderful letter about how he missed our talks and missed the friendship we had created. We continued our friendship after his letter, eventually leading to my finally asking him whether or not he ever thought about dating me, and the answer from him was yes! Finally! We went on our first date that weekend, got engaged eleven months later, and married one year later.

I still work at the library and thank my stars everyday that he walked through those front doors. I truly had—and still continue to have—the romance of my life at my local library.

Mary's Story

Although we met briefly at the mailbox, it was James's volunteer work at my branch library that won my heart. The library was in a retirement community, and he and I were still in our twenties. Both the library patrons and the staff were forty to fifty years older than we were, even the pages. It was such a breath of fresh air to have James around, always eager to help, especially with the heavy lifting—moving shelves, shifting books, whatever was needed. Yes, whatever was needed.

I heard a shriek once in the back corner. A snake had found its way into our library. "Oh James," I said, "Whatever shall we do?" Before I had time to contemplate our options, James had lifted the snake with his bare hands and both of them exited the library. I never saw the snake again.

But James . . . we gave him a pin at our volunteer recognition ceremony. And then I married him!

Kylie's Story

My partner, Andrew, and I are both librarians who work at the same Australian library, but the story of how we first met is a bit unusual.

I was working my first weekend shift—in our library, if you drive to work then you can collect a parking card, which permits staff to park in a special caged-in area of the parking lot. I collected my card, drove down to the parking lot, and parked my car. There is an elevator which goes up to the library. I went over, and this guy was standing there. I introduced myself, explaining that this was the first time that I had used the cage, and would he mind if I followed him? We went up to the library, through the staff entrance, and up the internal elevator, both getting out on the same floor. I thought to myself as I went to music and he to science, what a nice guy. So friendly and helpful; what a nice librarian!

Later on, Andrew's contract ended, and we both tried to look each other up. With very common surnames—Black and Smith!—it's tricky to just look us up in the phone book!

Fortunately, Andrew got another contract at the library. I found this out when, on my usual night shift in music, I thought that I saw Andrew on the science desk on the other side of the floor. Andrew obviously recognized me—he found two music books that belonged on my side, and used that as an excuse to come over and say hello. Quite a lengthy hello, in fact . . . luckily, there weren't many reference questions that night. We left for the caged parking lot together, discussing when we were next working. We did quite a few Tuesday nights together, and saw each other around the library and sent a few e-mails (mostly about cricket—this was when Australia was doing really well in the World Cup) and found that we had lots in common. A few weeks later we found that we were both working on the next Sunday afternoon. I resolved to ask him out for a drink after work, as it was looking inevitable by then. My opportunity came when he wrote DDATIWD at the end of an e-mail. I asked what it stood for; although he wrote back, he didn't explain. In my reply, I asked again, and said that if it has anything to do with going for a coffee after work, then I'm all for it! He accepted. (It's Don't Do Anything That I Wouldn't Do.)

We had a fabulous two-and-a-half-hour coffee. We have been living together for sixteen months and generally acting like we've been together for ages. We still work together, but have a rule of not talking about work at home. But we do have an enormous collection of books!!

Ann's Story

I had just turned sixteen when I started my first job at the Trenton Public Library in Trenton, New Jersey. Recovering from a bad case of poison ivy on my face, I was reluctant to meet the rest of the shelving staff, all of whom were male; but when I was sent down to the basement my future husband was standing by his locker at the foot of the steps and I couldn't avoid him. He claims he was immediately smitten, and didn't notice my lotion-covered patches of poison ivy rash. In subsequent weeks he left me comic poems and letters to discover when I shelved magazines in the stacks, and would often pop up from the floor below in the space next to the stack walkway to engage me in conversation. I wasn't yet allowed to date, but after some months, my mother, reassured by his respectable job at the library, relented and allowed me to go out. Seven years later we were married—that was forty years ago.

The Us Story—Simon Smith

I didn't know I was going to meet my future wife when I answered the door at the library in September 2002. Maybe if I had I would have worn a nicer shirt, as I thought she was beautiful. It was her first day and I welcomed her and took her upstairs while I went to find her new manager, and singularly failed to do so for about fifteen minutes. Feeling that this had made me look fairly foolish, we didn't speak again for about a month.

When we did have a chat it was a couple of minutes before an exciting staff briefing, so we didn't have very much time to say anything beyond, "How's it going?" and "Fine."

A few more weeks and nothing else—then we had a shared hour on the information desk, quite a rare occurrence, as we usually worked on different floors. We sat back to back but occasionally turned to face each other and talk, mainly about catalog searches and interlibrary loans.

Shortly afterward, the library closed for a month for a reorganization. Almost everything in the building had to be moved, so there were lots of tasks, and most of them required more than one pair of hands. For the first week, frustratingly, we were both carrying out different jobs in different parts of the building. After about a week, we were both assigned the tasks of shifting boxes of prospectuses, then moving some books. At one point, while I was shifting a video stand I looked up and saw her walking toward me, and thought that we were going to work together again. She told me that she had been sent down to relieve me, and I had to go upstairs. I felt fairly crushed.

Just before Christmas, the library staff party was held in part of the building, and we finally got the chance for a chat. We had another chat, then one that lasted a very long time. Unfortunately, just as we started to get on very well, Madeleine said that she'd probably have to go soon as she had to get the train back to Oxford, which was quite upsetting. Happily one of my housemates suggested that she stay over with us, and she agreed, so we had another few hours together. At the end of the party we walked from the library to the taxi stand, sharing an umbrella and feeling happy.

After getting home, we talked for hours. We found that we had both been thinking about each other, we had both wanted to talk, and each shared experience had been something that both of us had noticed and held on to. We had quite a bit in common and we enjoyed each other's company. Finally, as the dawn birdsong was starting and the sky was becoming lighter, we headed upstairs, initially for Madeleine to sleep on the floor of someone's room—but I invited her into mine.

A matter of hours later, we declared our love for each other. We didn't see each other for a week over Christmas but phoned more and more frequently, for longer and longer. A few weeks later, we moved into a new house together, and then three months after the Christmas party, we got engaged—our marriage happening just over a year later in April 2004.

We both still work at the same library, we still walk in every day, and we are still incredibly grateful that we found each other, something which certainly wouldn't have happened if it weren't for quirks of fate, geography, and most importantly, libraries—Reading Central Library in particular.

Kirsty's Story

It was a spectacularly boring day, the usual dull and dismal weather, very little to do. I was casually ambling down the stairs on my way to fetch a book for our only reader. I was miles away in thought, when I heard the ground floor doors fly open; Mark came bounding gazelle-like up the stairs with a kettle in his hand, tripped, fell up the last few stairs, and to my surprise, crash-landed at my feet! The contents of the kettle were of course contents no more, and before the kettle lid had rattled its last death throes, Mark had asked me out. I accepted almost automatically and we've been together ever since, some thirteen years now.

Our song is "Hungry Eyes" by Eric Carmen. It has fantastic lyrics and it was in one of the first films that we ever watched together. Of course Mark thought he looked like Patrick Swayze, as did everyone else at the time!

Hollie's Story

I work for Sirsi Corporation, a library automation software company, as a software trainer. In September 2003 Nick attended a class I was training in our Huntsville, Alabama, office. He works for Cedar Rapids Public Library as a person responsible for their network and computer systems and was sent to my class as a backup administrator for our software. I was interested in him immediately but had to keep everything strictly businesslike as he is a customer of ours. We had the opportunity to visit socially a couple of nights during the week he was in Huntsville and I knew without doubt that he was someone that I wanted to spend more time with, but I couldn't imagine how this would work with him in Iowa and me in Alabama. At the end of the week, Nick and I were on the same flight out of Huntsville and sat together on the plane. The ride to Atlanta was great and I couldn't believe that this was the end of our time together. I was devastated when we parted there. Nick came through though! On the following Monday, he e-mailed me and from that point on we never let a day pass without communicating either via e-mail or phone. We met in St. Louis one month later and had our official first date.

At this point, I became positive that Nick was the one! As if fate were in control, the week after our time together in St. Louis I was given a four-week assignment to train a library system in Iowa! This was very strange yet perfect timing. This allowed Nick and me to spend five weekends straight together and we used this time to date and get to know each other. Nick was able to visit Alabama again for the holidays and my travel schedule after New Year's allowed us to see each other at least twice a month. In February he asked me to move to Iowa and in May he proposed to me while on a business trip with me to Hawaii (which was also an assignment to train a library!).

The wedding was perfect—my dream wedding come true! We were married on December 4, 2004, in St. Louis, which was our meeting point when we were dating long distance! The wedding took place in a church located around the corner from the restaurant where Nick and I had our first date and then the reception was a trip down the Mississippi on a riverboat. We danced the night away to Dixieland jazz. After the wedding we took a little honeymoon down to New Orleans and then ran ourselves ragged visiting family for the holidays. We are now settled in Cedar Rapids and happier than ever! It is taking a little while for me to get used to the cold weather though! For Christmas Nick surprised me with a puppy. So we have now started our own little family with a three-pound beagle puppy named Zoey.

To sum up, the library world brought us together, allowed us to travel all over the United States to keep our relationship strong, *and* provided the most romantic setting for a proposal in Hawaii! Who knew working could make two people so happy! Thanks to Sirsi Corporation, Cedar Rapids Public Library, and all the other stops that have brought us this far!

Eva's Story[1]

Daniel and Eva were both working as librarians, but not at the same library. One day, fate and the EBSCO Company intervened. Fresh-faced, earnest librarians like Dan and Eva are in high demand for any number of thankless tasks at most libraries, like the EBSCO focus group that convened at the end of 2001. EBSCO wanted to know how to make their information databases more pleasant for real people to use.

Alike, but different, Eva and Daniel both went to small liberal arts colleges. They both studied Russian. They both played musical instruments. They both had complete sets of Mark Twain's books. They had both lived in Boston. They both had bad hair in the eighties (Okay, who didn't?). And, of course, they both went to library school at Big Ten universities in the Midwest.

As is Eva's custom, she arrived late. There was one empty seat, right next to Daniel. It could have been the clever points Eva made about how no amount of design can overcome bad indexing or how a user interface should be its own best tutorial. Or it could have been the chairs, which were so arranged that Eva nearly had to climb over the back of hers to sit down. But, at the break, Daniel offered her his business card. "Maybe we should get together some time, have coffee, talk about library stuff," he suggested, friendly and shy all at once. So began a slow but steady courtship, with Eva nursing old heartaches and proving to be a tough customer, while Daniel remained ever optimistic, patient, and sure.

Guess who was right? There are many kinds of love, but none is sweeter than being with someone who grows in your esteem every single day and makes you feel you've finally come home. High on Daniel and Eva's short list of serious commitments to make this year is adopting a scrappy dog. They'll almost certainly name him Ebsco.

The Change—Rodney Eloy and Marcia Regina

We had always heard that the year 2000 would be significant in many aspects and full of great happenings, which would leave a mark in time for some, or else it would be an end. For Marcia and Rodney it was about a big beginning, something spectacular and exciting.

These two young people, who live in a big city called São Paulo, Brazil, where many people meet and miss one another, had their lives changed by a very special surprise, something we can name, in this narrative, as being a great blessing.

In the beginning of the year 2000, I, Marcia, was trying to get into business again, when finally, with the help of a friend of mine, I found out that I could apply for a job vacancy at one of the many universities in the city.

I had faith and, in spite of some difficulties, I handed in my curriculum vitae. Certainly, there was a celestial purpose in my application, because on that day, February 16, 2000, the very best thing happened to me. Without being called for an interview, I was hired immediately to work in one of the sections of the university: the library.

From the beginning I made some friends, and among them there was Rodney, a smart, handsome, and sensitive boy, but we rarely had conversation. In the first months, our schedules didn't match and we met only a few times in that section. When it happened, our intention was not to flirt with each other; I just put some questions about the work to him. We both were carrying on with our lives and we didn't know anything about each other.

Five months had passed and the Central Library, which played a very important role on this story, had suffered some changes because the building was being renovated, and it was at that moment when everything began for us.

Due to school vacation, during the renovation, library service was stopped, and because of that, the entire library staff became very close to one another, participating in everything that was necessary, in a very friendly atmosphere. In the relaxed setting at this time, friendships were getting tighter; conversation became more intimate and glances more intense.

And then it dawned on me: Rodney and I couldn't explain what we were feeling; we only knew that our will to be together was getting stronger as the days went by.

Our curious glances many times met, darted away, got close again. Conversation started to take place, and we shared jokes, smiles, touches, and only one thought—to be close.

We waited excitedly for the sunrise, in order to meet at work. By this time, we started to plan trips and in every date there was a discovery, a new emotion.

One week, we planned to see Verdi's opera *Alzira* at the Teatro Municipal. On that unforgettable night, in an illuminated setting in downtown São Paulo, we definitely realized that we couldn't hide our feelings anymore, we were meant to be together, and we had very original witnesses to our love, full of important stories to tell us—books.

This date was marked with our first kiss and the certainty of the great love that had sprung in our hearts.

Time has passed; we still work together and discover, day by day, that we were united by exclusive reasons that make us a couple. We still live our story intensely, we are married and happy, and the library is still our special comrade. And, between one collection or another, our glances meet, every day more in love.

Note

1. www.bookoflove.us/daneva/html.

CHAPTER ELEVEN

The Romance of Library School

Library school is the source of many a romance. Perhaps the pressure cooker atmosphere of completing a library degree in order to get right into the inner workings of the library world intensifies the emotions. Library school may attract people with similar interests, values, and career goals, but it doesn't necessarily follow that the students in a particular class are one homogenous group. The great thing about the library world is that it attracts such a diversity of personalities, backgrounds, and interests.

Pecan Logs and Leonard Cohen—
Carrie-Ann Smith

I was on my way to library school in Halifax, Nova Scotia, where I had no apartment waiting for me, no friends, and not enough money to guarantee either one. Considering it looked like I might end up living in my car it was probably misguided to have packed as much in it as possible. The night before I left I "tarped" all of my worldly possessions into the trunk of my 1969 Plymouth Valiant and affixed blue and purple bungee cords in a symmetric design.

With Squeeze in the tape deck and tearful good-byes behind me, I drove for two days, taking a shortcut through the States. It had all been smooth sailing and my confidence was rising with the mileage on the gauge. There would actually be a momentary flash of panic a day later when I saw the Edmundston sign and thought that one, I had driven in the wrong direction, and two, that Edmonton was spelled wrong on what looked like a government-issued sign. But for the moment I was coming up on the Maine-New Brunswick border and feeling pretty good about myself. I should have known better.

All smiles, I pulled up to the border guard, a woman who hated me instantly. I wasn't fazed. I was a Canadian border town kid. I knew how to sit still in three pairs of pants and four back-to-school sweaters with fireworks tucked under my ass. In a lone pair of jeans with no ill-gotten American booty this would be a breeze. I answered every question honestly and politely but was unsurprised when she asked me to pull over and open the trunk. Open the trunk? It would have been easier to get American citizenship. Everything that I owned had been strategically placed in a giant Jenga game of personal history; it would never go back in.

As she wheeled over a double-decker autopsy table I mopped the sweat on my brow. The airport scene from *Midnight Express* kept flashing through my mind: don't sweat, do not sweat, stop sweating like a drug mule. Library school, I had told her I was on my way to library school—it sounded so fake. The guard and I approached the trunk and I unfastened the cords. She folded back the tarp revealing three white bundles.

"What are those?" she asked.

"I swear, I have never seen them before."

She picked up one of the mysterious bundles and silently read the love note from my mother that was wrapping one of my favorite childhood treats, a marshmallow-filled pecan log.

With a reluctant smile she said, "Fasten it back up and you can go."

While I was spending my last night in the house that I had grown up in, my mother had slipped out to the car, reached under the tarp, and hidden three pecan logs, gift-wrapped in notes that said things like, "I am so proud of you, my special girl."

Saved by pecan logs, I was soon back on the road and made it to Halifax. I didn't end up being homeless; I started school, and tried to make friends. I was lonely by the time classes started so on the first day I asked everybody I met if they wanted to go to a movie. I told all of them that I had a huge car and where I would be half an hour before show time. It was library school so the girl to guy ratio was about eight to one. Nonetheless, when I showed up at the appointed time and place there were four boys and no girls. Math had failed me again.

Among them was Peter; in the odd world of library school he was the male with the most romantic potential. He was a nonpracticing lawyer—which was impressive and intriguing. He had great hair that naturally fell into a Superman-like curl at the front. He was gorgeous, so I figured that between the good looks and brains that he was wildly out of my league. I couldn't even claim new-girl cachet because it was the first day of classes and we were all new girls. I drove everyone home after the movie, saving Peter for last. He invited me in to see his apartment, giving me the impression that it was quickly turning into a bona fide date. After a hello to his roommate and a short walk down the hall, he then opened the door to reveal a bedroom entirely furnished in black. Furnished in black is an understatement. Every item in the room, even the few items of visible clothing, was black. Then I saw it, a framed photograph of Leonard Cohen.

I had a favorite little black dress and liked a couple of sad songs but Peter had taken it up a notch and showed all signs of being a party girl's nightmare. It was the equivalent of a guy walking into a girl's dorm room looking for a good time and finding not just a copy of *The Bell Jar* but a portrait of Sylvia Plath. It didn't matter anyway because he then walked me through the rest of the two-bedroom apartment and then back to my car—he didn't think it was a date at all. The bastard was just being polite. Of all the nerve.

So romance would elude me for the moment but I had my first library school friends. I sat in the back of the classrooms with the guys and we did most of our group work together. In any other environment I would have been the conservative one but it wasn't very hard to be a badass in the working collection. I met my best friend on a frosh harbor cruise. She was in the geology department so I began to date my way through the life science building. Boys in hiking boots and shorts all year round hold an uncommon allure. Through picking me up at school, located on the third floor of the Killam Library, my geologist friend encountered all of my classmates. Although the males held no allure for her she had to acknowledge that Peter was handsome and brilliant but that his total lack of interest in me was unforgivable. She

hated him on my behalf and we took to calling him the Dark Lord or
the Byronic hero of library school.

The first year and a half of library school passed. I wrote "Girls Just
Want to Have Fonds" for archival studies, took every opportunity possible to condemn the theory that teams produce better results than indi-
viduals, and waited patiently for a chance to use what I considered to
be my undergraduate masterpiece, a graphic study of Victorian pornog-
raphy. There were papers, parties, geologists, impounded cars, and
pecan log-filled care packages from northern Ontario. Then came a
late October day in 1995.

It was the rare kind of day that unites summer people and winter
people in unanimous agreement on its perfection. It was sunny and
warm but the promise of Thanksgiving turkey and Christmas presents
was hinted at in the breeze. My car had died the previous night and I
was forced to walk to school. Any other day this would have put me in
a foul mood but it was so lovely that I had my denim jacket tied around
the waist of my dress and there was something empowering about the
way its weight made my stride feel like a sway.

I had walked for about fifteen minutes when I came to a train bridge.
It was just a piece of street with a concrete railing on either side and
train tracks underneath ferrying cargo, little noticed from above. On
my side of the bridge there was a young man standing on the wide rail.
I gave him a big smile, as one in a swishy dress is wont to do on a sunny
day. His stance on the rail struck me as odd but I didn't think much of
it. It was the kind of day that makes old men whistle as they walk and
young men drive with the windows down and the stereo blaring so
standing on a bridge made sense where maybe it wouldn't have in the
rain.

I had reached the end of the bridge and had just started to cross in
front of a truck on a little side street when the driver of the truck called
me over.

"Did you see the boy on the bridge?" he said. "He is going to jump,
you know, he is just waiting for the train."

"When is the train coming?"

"Any minute now."

I walked back to the bridge with absolutely no clue what to do or
say. My entire experience with suicide, I am happy to report, had been

situation comedy scenarios which always ended up with everybody who tried to help out on the ledge of a tall building. There was no ledge, no guest star, I had nothing. I relied on my limited gift for small talk and my silent prayers that I wouldn't hear the train. It was probably just a few minutes before my guest star showed up. The man in the truck had sent in reinforcement in the form of a good-looking guy around my age and he was a fast talker.

"Come on down and we'll all go get some food," he was saying. "Come on, me and this girl want to buy you lunch."

Nothing, the boy wasn't even looking at us as we stared up, talking fast and not getting through. We didn't notice the two policemen approaching but in a matter of seconds one had jumped up, wrapped his arms around the boy and hauled him down. He put him in the police car while his partner stayed behind to ask us questions. Two friends joined my partner in distraction as the policeman asked us how we had come to be on the bridge and if the boy had said anything. The three men seemed to know the officer and were joking around with him the way people do when they are nervous or uncomfortable and reluctant to show it.

When the police left the four of us just stood there, stunned by the events of the previous few minutes as the train passed underneath. They invited me to lunch; after what had just happened, getting into a car with three total strangers made perfect sense. We sat in a booth at a neighborhood cafe and ordered four identical meals, eating in almost total silence. The quiet was broken when one of their cell phones rang. All three of them had to check their phones, which was comical, and grew increasingly so as our meal was constantly interrupted by ringing and hands flying into pockets and raising tiny phones for cryptic conversations. It was on about the fourth ring that I finally put their familiarity with the policeman together with the calls and realized that they were probably drug dealers—nice guys, who insisted on picking up the tab for my lunch and driving me to campus, but drug dealers nonetheless.

A suicide intervention, police questioning, and lunch with well-meaning underworld types all in the space of an hour. By the time that my companions dropped me off I was ready to tell the story to the first person that I bumped into. It happened that Peter's was the only familiar face that I saw. Peter, the brooding Byronic hero of library school, the black-wearing, Leonard Cohen–listening, painfully good-looking embodiment of everything that I hated. He would have to do.

"I had a surreal walk to school; can I buy you a coffee and tell you about it?"

"Okay."

I told the story at greater length than I am imparting it here and he listened attentively. He told a story and then I told another. We went on that way for hours. It was the first real conversation that we had ever had. At one point I mentioned that I would not be going home for Christmas because I had to stay in Halifax and complete my practicum for school. I was just making conversation but he ended up asking me if I wanted to spend Christmas with his family. Caught up in the conversation and genuinely grateful for the thoughtfulness of the invitation, I said yes.

When I got home that night I called my geologist friend and told her the whole story of the day culminating in the holiday invitation. I remember what she said exactly: "Don't tell me anything that is going to make me like him." I couldn't help it; I was warming up to him and she was going to have to go along for the ride. For better or for worse, I was going to see what sort of environment produced Peter. I couldn't imagine. I would go more out of morbid curiosity than anything else.

Peter picked me up in the afternoon on Christmas Eve day and we drove for half an hour into the country. I had an eye out for a black house, maybe a yard full of black cars, but we pulled into the driveway of a beautiful country house tucked into Saint Margaret's Bay. It turned out to be the rectory for his father's Anglican parish. What the hell? It got even better: his mom was super nice, his siblings were freakishly normal, and there were little kids running around hopped up on sugar and excited about Santa. Worlds were colliding and I was at the point of impact; it smelled like turkey and good will, which was weird. Later that night, after everyone had gone to bed, I found myself on the sofa with the Dark Lord.

"Do you want to watch a movie?"

"Okay."

What would it be? What would it be? I was trying desperately not to like him and felt pretty confident that his film choice would give me resolve. He got up, put the film in, and rejoined me on the couch as *The Secret Garden* began. Peter was showing me freaking *The Secret Garden* on Christmas Eve in his parents' rectory. I was back in "what the hell?" mode when he leaned in for what looked like it was going to be a kiss. Yep, it was a kiss, a good one, followed by a declaration of affection which I had no power to resist. Eighteen months later we were married.

In the last eight years we have had pecan logs mailed to us by my mother on every major holiday, hung the portrait of Leonard Cohen in three different houses, and wondered about what happened to the boy on the bridge often. I always say that no one can accuse me of going to library school to find a husband. No one goes to library school looking for romance but that doesn't mean it may not be looking for you.

Susanne's Story

My husband and I met in the spring of 1997 in my very first library class, Introduction to Library and Information Science, at the University of Texas at Austin. The funny thing is that he wasn't a library student, but an architecture student who was taking this class as an elective. Someone had (mistakenly) told him that it would be a good class for learning how to improve your research skills. All he got out of it was meeting me. Although we were both involved with other people when we first met at the beginning of the semester, we were both conveniently uninvolved by the end of the semester. Our first official date was a few days after the class final. We were married in November of 2000.

Denise's Story

I met Steve at Kent State University School of Library Science. We met in the study room/lounge area for the library school students near the school offices, the classrooms, and the library studies book collections. I remember we noticed each other, then started chatting over coffee one day and hanging out with mutual friends. At that time he was a bearded, dark-haired tweedy type that smoked a pipe and wanted to be a history bibliographer. That dusty small student lounge was where he first put his arm around my shoulders on a dare from a fellow student with a camera. I still have the picture of us grinning and making eyes at each other snuggled up on an old couch. We hit it off big time and were soon going to movies, eating meals together, and sharing a typewriter.

We married about two years later and divorced four years after that. Libraries didn't play a big part in our marriage as romantic settings. But career pressures were a factor in our split. We were both ambitious and it was very hard to find two good jobs in academic libraries in the same city. For a year Stephen worked part time in a job he disliked to be with me. The relationship never recovered from that stress. We divorced without a lot of nastiness or arguments.

Lori's Story

I met my husband in library school at Emporia State University, Emporia, Kansas. I started the program a semester after he did, so it was a couple of semesters later that we had a class together. I had been living in Lawrence, Kansas, for two years (having moved from northern Illinois), and was commuting to Emporia three days a week (an eighty-mile trip each way). Nick had been in Kansas for one year. He came there from Cherkassy, Ukraine. I later found out that the only reason he enrolled as a student was that his visa required that he be a student in order to stay in the United States. Library science was the closest thing ESU offered to the patent law degree he had received in the Ukraine. The class that brought us together was one on reference resources. We had to get into groups and do a presentation on one type of resource. At this point, we knew each other's names, but thought the other one wasn't available. Nick assumed I was married and I thought he was married, since he was wearing a wedding ring. When we ended up in the same group, he discovered that I had never been married, and Nick was divorced, but hadn't taken off the ring. We had our first "official" date on March 13, 1993, and were married March 19, 1994 (which was during spring break). It was love at second date for us, because that's when we started talking about marriage.

To make matters even more interesting, we are both librarians at Salina Public Library in Salina, Kansas. I am a reference librarian, and

Nick is the cataloger. We've been coworkers for ten years. Most people ask us how we can stand working with our spouse, but we just tell them it's great! Besides, we only have to take one car to work in the morning! So, if it weren't for libraries, our love of books, and Emporia State University, we wouldn't have met at all.

Jerry's Story

My wife and I met at the University of Iowa Main Library in 1986. Everybody in our selection class (in one of the library school's classrooms at the south end of the library's third floor) formally introduced themselves, but I consider our real meeting to have been by the journal room copier (also on the third floor) one night when we were both working on a class assignment. I don't remember where the topics of conversation went after the assignment, but we ended up at the steps of her dorm about a mile away, leaving me about ten minutes to run back that mile to catch the last bus out to my apartment (yes, I made it). I asked her out a couple weeks after that; marriage came about a year and a half later, a week after I got my MLS from Illinois (I wasn't formally in the Iowa program).

Neither of us had a job when we married, but we both had interviews scheduled for the week after the honeymoon. We gave the travel agent a turn when we bought a ticket for me to Dayton, Ohio, and for Kathy to Cheyenne, Wyoming, and said something about getting married in two days. Both interviews were successful, but we decided that Kathy's job and my prospects were better in Cheyenne than my job and her prospects in Wilmington, a small college town east of Dayton. Kathy is now the Wyoming state law librarian, and I'm the medical librarian for Poudre Valley Health System in Fort Collins, Colorado (about forty-five miles south of Cheyenne).

Robin's[1] Story

My husband and I didn't exactly meet in a library, but I think it would qualify as a library-related setting. We also went through library school together. He was an assistant manager for a now-defunct independent bookstore when I began working there, when I was fresh out of college with an English degree and no other employment prospects. On my first day of work, he took me on the grand tour, including going through each section (which was more difficult than learning one's way around a library, not being organized by Dewey or Library of Congress). I liked the way he looked in his crisp white button-down shirt, as well as his overall demeanor. Later on he helped me tune my guitar, and then we found ourselves mourning the loss of our state's great guitar legend, Stevie Ray Vaughn. Not long after, he quit the bookstore in hopes of making more money in sales. A little while later I got a call from him, and we started going out.

His career in sales was short-lived, and we both started to think about the possibility of becoming librarians instead. We applied to a nearby university and were accepted into their graduate school of library and Information sciences. We commuted together and went to area libraries together to do our research. After graduation, we broke up for a few months. I took a special library job in another state. He came to visit, and finally convinced me that we belonged together. The shortage of library jobs in this area led him into management with a bookstore chain and eventually into starting our own online bookstore, which he now does full time. I still work in a library though.

Mark's Story

I met my wife while we were both studying for a master's in librarianship at Sheffield University, Department of Information Studies, in the UK. When I was registering with my new house mates at the university in my first week in Sheffield, our long queue wasn't moving, so I took a few seconds to sort out another form or two. When I came back the line had moved on and being too polite to push past and cut in at my rightful place I chickened out and joined at the back of the same line, slightly longer. Overcome with the euphoria of being a new person in a new place I chose to drop my general sullen disposition in lieu of a friendlier persona. I struck up conversation with a petite good-looking blue-eyed blonde directly in front of me; I might add that I would have struck up conversation even if the person in front of me had been a bearded fifty-year-old physics student. We got chatting; I asked her what course she was on and . . .

I'm now editor of the *Public Library Journal* and a community librarian, Stamford Group, and my beautiful wife Amanda is a community librarian, Grantham, so we both currently work for the same county library service—Lincolnshire. We've been married almost two years now and she hasn't returned me yet.

Amanda calls us the Posh and Becks of the library world, but I think we earn slightly less; Amanda has a great voice though I'm all out of tattoos. We have one child—a black Labrador called Bessie.

Sandra's Story

My husband Mark and I met at the University of British Columbia's School of Library, Archives and Information Studies (SLAIS). We always sat on opposite sides of the room—myself near the door and he on the far side of the room near the windows. Considering that we never worked on projects together or sat near each other, I am sometimes amazed we even hooked up. But we did. We started e-mailing each other—we still have a stack of e-mail printouts (at least an inch) of the e-mails we sent each other that document our getting to know each other. Self-important, I know, but they're significant to us because that's really how our relationship started as we were both so busy with school, work, and volunteering. It had only been a few months when we found ourselves facing graduation and the only thing we wanted— aside from finding meaningful work—was to stay together. We decided to leave the Vancouver region because, at that time, the job market wasn't ideal for such a large graduating class and the odds of us both finding work beyond auxiliary weren't great. We found contract work in Alberta, but nothing that allowed us to feel like we belonged to an organization. So we decided to take the plunge and head south of the border.

When Mark and I were looking for work in the United States we saw two positions at the same public library in Texas (one cataloging and one business reference), which were perfect for our skill sets. We decided to apply by sending both of our resumes under one cover letter so they knew we were a package deal. They interviewed us both over the phone (same phone call) and, soon after, offered us the positions. The situation was perfect. We couldn't have gone down together otherwise because of the way that the North American Free Trade Agreement works: if only one of us had gotten a position there, the other one couldn't have simply started working. So our situation was perfect. For a while, we worked on different floors of the same public library in Texas and wowed patrons with our foresight into their information needs (thanks to the wonders of interdepartmental phone lines).

One of the great things about being a librarian couple is that we always get the apartments we apply for, border crossing is pretty painless, and banks seem to like us (knock wood!). I guess it is beyond people's imaginations that librarians could be rowdy or dishonest—and two together are just double the goodness. But then the librarians I know are honest and hard-working so I think that, in general, we tend to live up to our positive stereotypes!

We are now back in the lower mainland of British Columbia: Mark is working as an academic liaison librarian and I'm in public library management. We like to say that we traveled across two provinces and two countries with our degrees before returning home—and we now have a little guy who may just be one of the smallest soon-to-be members of the British Columbia Library Association.

J. K. and Manju's Story

We met in the library school of a residential university located in southern India. It was in 1994 that we registered for bachelor's degrees in library and information science; we were only good friends then. Next year we enrolled for master's degrees where the intake was just twelve, and there we fell in love. We kept it as a top secret for the entire academic year and revealed it to our friends at the end. Then we moved to our native state, where J. K. registered for professional training and Manju for an IT course. In 1997 we got married, and in 1998 we shifted to another state in western India.

Now we have a baby girl, and we will try our level best to make her a librarian.

Heather's Story

Given the ratio of males to females, I never expected to fall in love in library school. But that's where Richard and I met. He, incidentally, saw the male/female ratio as a blessing. Richard and I have been together for almost four years, since the fall of our first year at Dalhousie School of Library and Information Studies. It was our first group project and I had teamed up with two friends. We were waiting for Richard to sign up for a group so that we could join him. We suspected he was a computer whiz and that his skills would come in handy. He took forever to put his name down, so we just asked him to join us. Later I found out he was waiting for *me* to sign up. We were just pals for a while. He was very quiet (then!).

Here comes the mush. One day we were sitting in a coffee shop and I looked up at him and noticed, for the first time, how blue his eyes were and that was it. Our first "date" was the annual Santa Claus parade, so we try to go each year to remember shivering in the cold together, enjoying the sights and good cheer of the parade, lights, and people around us. Of course, our most frequent gift to each other is books, though we read very different types of literature! It is nice to find a fellow willing to snuggle up with you—and a good book!

Since we couldn't find jobs in the same place, we've been maintaining a long distance relationship. But we hope to be in the same city again within the next year or so and eventually get married. Of course, we will be inviting all of our library school pals to celebrate with us.

Eloise's[2] Story

[The following story isn't exactly about romance, but it is about relationships and shared values.]

Have you ever felt compelled to quell your curiosity about someone else, and had the answers change you forever?

I started attending library school full time at a rural college in southern New England in the late 1980s. At age thirty-one, I was in a solid romantic relationship with a woman who lived about four hours drive north but, working as a children's librarian and educator, I was accustomed to being in the closet professionally about my lesbian lifestyle. I had come to study full time, and was resigned to being closeted and quite possibly the only gay person in my program during the year to come. Then, about halfway through the short summer semester, I ran into Barbra, a woman who made my internal "gaydar" system beep like a circulation alarm gone mad. She had the walk, the hair, and the watchful manner of handling personal questions that becomes almost second nature to many people who live in deeply separated public and private worlds. Of course I recognized that—it was exactly the way I felt. I restrained myself from making assumptions though, because if my "gaydar" was wrong, I could be opening a moldy pile of books coming out to her, risking the possibility of her outing me later to people in the children's librarianship program, thus compromising my ability to do well there and find a job afterward, as public gays and lesbians were not (and sadly, are still not) welcome in most school settings in the United States.

So I kept mum, and tried to find ways of getting to know this woman—no easy task, as while she seemed happy to be befriended, she was naturally shy even beyond her learned reticence. I would analyze each small crumb of personal information I managed to pull from her, weighing, wondering, not daring to say anything to her about myself.

My sense of cultural isolation built with each day that passed in that very straight program, despite covert phone calls to my sweetie, who was a loving but distant two-hundred-plus miles away. If only I could talk honestly with someone here—it would be so good to have even just one other like-minded person in the program. What about that Barbra, anyways?

Then, one Friday afternoon, in the computer lab, my carefully constructed silence crumbled. Barbra and I were there along with some other students and when the others left, and my need to know overcame my caution—I just had to find out, one way or the other. Our extraordinarily suave and sophisticated conversation went something like this:

Eloise: (waves) Hi, Barbra.

Barbra: (approaching Eloise's cubby) Hi, Eloise. How are you?

Eloise: (breaking eye contact) Ahh, I'm fine. (Overly casual) Hey, I just wondered . . . are you gay? (holds breath and monitors Barbra's face intently, watching at the same time for the nearest exit)

Barbra: (pauses, looks around for escape routes, turning several interesting skin shades from palest ivory to bright red) Unnh . . . well . . . ummmm. . . . (suddenly direct and on the defensive) yeah, I am.

Eloise: (breathing out at last) Oh, good; I am too.

Barbra: (face brightening, also breathing hugely) Really? Am I glad to hear it!

For the rest of the afternoon we discussed (in near whispers) our "lesbrarian" lives and experiences, and a friendship was born that lasted from our first gay alliance meeting in September (still a fairly radical notion back then) through graduation, job searches, girlfriends, and other life changes. Fifteen years later we are still in touch, still comparing notes on libraries, literature, and life. Lesbrarians forever!

Fiona's Story

It was the first day of library school at Curtin University in Western Australia. I had actually enrolled the year before (1995) but it was too much as my kids were a bit too little, so I deferred to 1996. I had been on my own for some time and, to be honest, had little income and this was a way to obtain some Austudy—financial help given by the government to help poor people study. Learning about how to obtain information really appealed to me.

We were all seated in a horseshoe arrangement of desks and had to stand up and say a little bit about ourselves. I remember thinking that that guy over on the other side was the only interesting one there. A couple of classes later I walked in and he was sitting on my side of the horseshoe (in the next seat to mine)!

Over the next three years of the degree we developed a very solid friendship and occasionally went to the coffee shop together. To me he was wise in some way and to him I was wise in some way. I used to get a bit disappointed if I didn't bump into him during the day. Once he said that he hadn't seen me for ages and put his hand on my arm (for more than the socially acceptable one second).

One day in 1999, there was a knock on my door and there he stood on my doorstep. We married in 2002. At first I was a bit upset that I'd lost this really great male friend as the relationship changed in its nature!

Today, he has a librarian position at a public library. He has been more successful than me in that he had experience before he got his degree. I did the degree without a foot in the door first and have found it difficult to enter the fairly closed workforce.

Not to worry, it's amazing how you can develop as a person! I got a job as a Christmas elf at one of the major department stores in western Australia—right body shape, cheery disposition, no adjustment needed to the ears.

James's[3] Story

In 1988 I was just emerging from a divorce after a thirty-year marriage. Most of the five kids were out of the house and it was time to part company. I also started teaching graduate library school that year.

In my second semester a charming woman entered my class late, which is why I noticed her. She did good work and was an active participant in class. Next semester she was in class again and interestingly she had to create a "library lesson" for elementary school and the format was a poster and talk entitled "Breakfast with James." That's my name. It was done in good fun.

The following semester, which was a one-week intense summer class, she was in my class again. At the beginning of the summer class, I asked each student to write a short biographical sketch about themselves, where they were in library school, and where they were heading. When the class was done, I had time to look them over. I was missing one, and it was just the one I wanted to read the most. I do this biographical exercise because students will often call me a few months or years later for a reference or recommendation. I find this helps. I am not being nosy.

Two days later, I received in the mail a note along with a biographical sketch from my favorite student. I was delighted. That was her last class and she was off to Disneyland. I think there was a TV commercial at the time, about finishing a baseball game or World Series or something and then going to Disneyland. She was taking her two children and camping all the way there.

In the fall I took a part-time job covering the desk in the children's room in a nearby public library on Sundays. I took the name plate out of the holder on the desk, turned it over, and pasted my name on a piece of paper and mounted it on the desk. It was only sometime later I realized whose name was on the other side—my favorite former student.

One evening I called that library for an interlibrary loan and who answered the phone? We struck up a conversation which has continued for the past fifteen years. Now I am full-time faculty and she is an adjunct. We have just celebrated the birth of our first grandchild (my step grandchild). We coteach classes at the library school and do an in-service course together for teachers.

Yes, you can find love in library school.

Alyson's Story

I studied for my first degree at Oxford University (1993–1996), and the Radcliffe Camera there was reputed to be a hotbed of passion, with little studying being done! However, my books were not in that amazing building, but in the New Library over the road, and nothing very exciting ever happened there. One friend who used to study in the "Rad Cam" (as it was known) used to come back to lunch in college describing some lovely girl he'd spied over the wooden barriers between desks. He never got anywhere with any of the women he saw there though!

Some people claimed to have seen/overheard couples becoming physical among the shelves of my college library, although I never saw anything myself (or did anything like that). My college library was accessible twenty-four hours a day though, so it's plausible!

I later came to use the Rad Cam as a visiting student for a few days. It was out of term time though and the library was very quiet, so there weren't many people to daydream about. However, the layout and the atmosphere of the building would be conducive to illicit romantic daydreams and encounters!

After studying for my degree, I then worked in a college library in Oxford for two years as the library assistant. The library was in an amazing building, a converted church, and I said at the time, "I'll never work in another library if it's not as beautiful as this," and that is true today! The students were a nice bunch, and because I was only just a bit older than them, I still felt connected to them. One group asked me to their special annual dinner, and I went, although I felt a bit out of place at the time. One of the girls asked me to go, but I think she was asking on behalf of a male student, although I don't know who he was. Earlier that year I had received a mystery Valentine's Day card delivered to me at the library, but there were no clues at all as to who the student was. It was very exciting though, receiving it through the internal mail system, and I happened to open it when I was at my desk in the library, which was visible to the students. I still wonder if the person who sent it was around at that moment to see me blush! I didn't have any actual romances while working at the library, but I did daydream about one Irish postgraduate. I think our sum total of conversations would amount to about five minutes, and all of those were about locating missing books, or helping him use the catalog. Not very exciting!

I then left Oxford and came to Aberystwyth, Wales, to go to library school. And it is here that I met my current partner. Quite early on in the first week of term, a gang of about ten of us formed around shared interests and over the next few weeks I found myself being drawn to one guy, Karl. When I found out he was vegan, my mind was made up! (I was a lapsed vegan at the time, but have since become vegan again.) After one very drunken night out with the group, we got together. The night had been planned in the pub the previous week and entailed us visiting everyone's house or room for a drink before moving on to the next house. We started off with chips in a local cafe, then proceeded to the first house, and the next, and so on. After leaving the last house I invited him back to my room, and we haven't looked back since! During that year, several other people got together on the course, but sadly three of those couples have split up, although they are happy with new partners.

Since finishing the course my partner got a job in the university library, and enjoys meeting the new intake of students each year! I meanwhile am doing a Ph.D., so I am still using libraries. I am also involved in some teaching of the library and information studies course to undergraduates. In my first year of teaching I received a mystery Valentine's Day card. Because of the way it was addressed to me I know it was from some students. I say "some" because they had altered the message to read "Be our Valentine" rather than "my" Valentine. I still don't know who they are, but it certainly brought a big grin to my face for weeks afterward. I smile now, to recall getting it.

Libraries have always played a big part in my life, and particularly for meeting my boyfriend! There is just something about the quietness of the place that emphasizes other actions, the other senses. They are great places for stealing a look at someone through the shelves or over the top of a book!

Heather's Story

I met Patrick in library school. Our first semester (fall 2000), we had three out of our four classes together. We worked together on a group project for human information behavior class: the topic was the reference interview. Our group ended up making a puppet show! After the project, Patrick and I continued to e-mail each other, first sharing our experiences juggling our new library jobs and library school classes, then we e-mailed about everything and became very close. Our second semester we had only one class together. We went out as friends. I thought it was a date, he thought we were just going out! Right as the semester was ending, Patrick worried that he wouldn't get to see me each week and called me to make special plans.

We graduated in January 2002. We decided to find professional jobs first and then work out the details of a wedding. We were married on November 2, 2002. We celebrated with only fifty guests. We invited a bunch of librarians to the wedding and even had a professional picture taken of all librarians present.

Patrick started feeling sick shortly after we were married. But we just thought he was getting old. He was about to turn thirty in May. By the summer, he was taking a lot of days off work. In July/August, Patrick started making many trips to different doctors. He was finally diagnosed with Hodgkin's disease on October 31, 2003. This cancer is supposed to be very curable, and we were told things like, "Don't worry, this is just an inconvenience . . . this is the best kind of cancer to get."

This isn't a story about cancer, but about librarian romances. Patrick was so ill, at times, I had to help him with his work. His employer was wonderful about letting him be sick, even before we knew what it was. I had quit my job and taken a part-time job in a local public library so I could spend more time taking Patrick to doctors and just caring for him at home.

In the meantime, a position opened up for a reference and instruction librarian at the library Patrick worked at. It was a dream job so I applied. The position then got changed and since he was so sick, I didn't bother reapplying. But they contacted me, so I had to interview. When they offered me the job, we were really surprised and really happy. Patrick's family medical leave was about to run out, so this was wonderful. We'd be able to have the same coverage so we could continue to see the same doctors.

But Patrick was getting sicker and sicker. We went to the hospital about ten days before I was to start my new job. We found out the chemotherapy wasn't killing his cancer at all . . . and with Hodgkin's disease if the chemo doesn't work, then you have to go for clinical trials. Patrick was too ill to face any of that. That time is very hard for me to remember. Patrick was in the hospital from January 15 to February 2. I started my new job on January 26. I worked one day. The doctors told me that it wasn't looking too good and that they had all the hope in the world . . . but there was nothing they could do. My husband was so delirious, so weak, so tired, and so sick. I don't know if he knew how sick he was. Patrick died early Monday, February 2, 2004. He was thirty, I was twenty-six.

For having a wedding only fifteen months earlier with fifty guests, I was surprised that well over a hundred and fifty people were at his funeral. I returned to work on February 10. I didn't have to go back right away, but I didn't really want to stay home. I needed something to do. It felt so good to be at his library, which is right next to the library school we attended. Everyone knew him and loved him. It still is very comforting to be around others who miss him too.

My time with Patrick was really short—he died two years and nine months after our first kiss; the day we feel we became official. But this time was the best of my entire life. It was just so wonderful to be married to someone with whom I shared so many common interests. It was so great having a husband who really cared about my work. We said that we loved libraries and librarians so much that we both became one and married one. He helped me organize my CD collection. He was more "techie" and worked with digital libraries. I love reference and instruction mostly. So our jobs were different, but our motivations similar.

Esther's Story

In 1991, at the age of twenty-one, I started at library school in the Netherlands. In a class of about thirty, there were only about three guys and one of those guys was Marcel, who was twenty at the time. It wasn't love at first sight. He was just one of the many students to me and I was just one of the many students to him. Also, both he and I were involved with other partners at the time, but those relationships ended not long after the school year started and we were both free to look around. Marcel and I were in the same group of friends and we were thrown together a lot; we starting really liking each other a lot.

At some point each of us tried to find a seat next to the other during classes; while we were studying in the school library we'd find seats at the same table; we'd start hanging out together after class drinking tea or coffee in the school canteen with a group of friends, and by the end of the afternoon just he and I would be left, chatting away.

When Christmas came around we sent each other Christmas cards with hidden love messages (mine said, "May all your wishes come true next year,"and all the while I was hoping that my wishes were the same as his). Then at the beginning of the New Year (1992), after dropping a million hints, Marcel asked me out on a date. We went dancing and on the morning of January 26, 1992, we finally kissed for the first time. We have been a couple ever since.

During library school we did a lot of projects together: we both went to England to do our internships in two separate libraries in the same city there. Our first job was a five-month project in a small library in Germany that we did together. In 1996 we both found jobs in libraries here in the Netherlands and we finally moved in together. We were married on July 26, 1999, our seven-and-a-half-year anniversary.

Marcel now works for the government where he is involved in digitizing government archives. I am now the head of a small college library. We have two wonderful children, a son born in July 2001 and a daughter born in December 2003. Our journeys toward entering that library school have been long and winding and we thank our lucky stars that we both ended up going there and finding each other there.

We played U2's "All I Want Is You" as our wedding dance song. We both love the song and the title just says it all.

Susan's Story

New to this large city last year, I came to the university for the library and information studies program. I was warned about criminals in the city, guys who are players and take advantage of girls. So I was very distant and blocked other people from getting too close to me and knowing anything about my love life or personal information.

At that time I was still talking to my best friend (also ex-boyfriend) from Vancouver, because he was the one I was closest to and listened to me the most. But I was ready to move on to a new relationship, sometimes being so desperate that I'd post my profile on five online websites for matchmaking or dating services, but with no luck finding an interested and decent guy who didn't want a one-night fling.

Then in the library school, there was a guy who was very open and friendly; he was very inviting and welcoming. He was a popular Bangladeshi guy who was surrounded by people from all sorts of backgrounds: Desi, Chinese, and Caucasians. People liked his company, his funny stories, and his unbelievable true stories. His chattiness, good sense of humor, and easygoing nature made him quite approachable, so that his peers liked to talk to him and sometimes seek him out for counseling, or having fun and hanging out with coffee. The best part was when he shared tasty cookies from his native country. Everyone liked having teatime with him and catching up on conversations. I, too, enjoyed his company, especially when he spent one-on-one time with me, because he was able to make me feel good about myself, laugh, and get personal attention. Although one thing that troubled me was that he talked to a lot of young women, flirted with them, and hung out with them. He struck me as a player and untrustworthy when it came to relationships. Many young women in school and some at his workplace were attracted to him. He was open, generous, charming, a good cook, and carefree, qualities that are different from some Canadians. Having lived in Canada for only three years, he seemed like a fresh person, exotic and spicy.

Slowly we got to know each other more, but I refused to give him too much personal information and let him get too close to me. As the months went by, I grew more interested in Indian culture, even though I am Taiwanese and usually the cultures don't mix. He e-mailed me frequently with teasing and flirty smiles, joking a lot about things. After five months, things picked up.

The first day he touched my hand was at the salsa dance. He stroked my fingers and interlocked them. I wasn't sure what to think of it: was he touching my hand because he had to hold them as my dance partner, or was he giving hints that he was interested in me? Stronger feelings developed. Sometimes he asked me about my past love life, or what I want in a guy, and I started to wonder whether he liked only me or if I was just one of the young women he talked to in school. Whenever he tried to find out more information about me, I would block him, pull back, and become cold. On and off it happened; we would have a good time, laugh, and joke around, but whenever I sensed he was getting closer or might have a crush on me, I would push him away. The whole cycle troubled and tormented him. Many times he got offended and thought of cutting off his friendship with me, and likewise I got annoyed by his prying and pushy nature.

By the summer 2004, we hung out more in a group, went out on trips, visited each other's place. Closer and closer we got, and my attraction for him deepened to the point that my resistance melted. One day he wanted to come over and talk; by then we were sure we liked each other, but I still hesitated. Finally I relented. He came over and smiled, he said he was happy just to be here with me. We talked little, because our emotions were stronger. Unable to withhold my feelings anymore, I went to him. We held hands, and sparks of electric thrill went through my body. I leaned on the nape of his neck, trying hard to stop myself from flinging myself at him, but I could not help it anymore. I'd had weeks of dreaming about him, sleepless nights, every day, hour, minute, spent thinking about him, about his gelled hair, his dimpled smile, and his smooth brown skin; gazing deep into his big, light brown eyes and dark perfect eyebrows; wanting to stroke his wide shoulders and muscular arms, to caress his soft shaved cheeks, to smell his manly scent. I was driving myself crazy. Our cheeks touched and we turned toward each other. Our lips finally met and we gave each other a long passionate kiss, full of excitement and affection. I stroked his hair and face, enjoying kissing his pink, soft, lovely lips. We spent that whole night talking, playing with each other's hands, feeling so happy and in love.

The next few days we were like lovesick birds. We talked more, caressed each other, content in each other's company. We forgot about our schoolwork and stopped e-mailing or talking to our friends on our cell phones. We were happy to be in our romantic bubble world.

Finally we tuned back in and answered calls and messages. His friends demanded to know what was happening, how come he was ignoring them. My mother called, suspecting something fishy was happening, despite her disapproval of my dating anyone. I bet she'd be shocked to find out I was going out with a guy, especially a Bangladeshi guy! His family inquired about what was wrong, why he did not contact them much anymore.

Despite being so in love, we had to enter reality again. After shouldering all the questions and suspicion, we were able to go out, eat at restaurants. We held hands while walking down the street, smiling at each other. He felt so proud he finally found a loyal and committed girlfriend that he felt like shouting to the world about the good news. Months of painstaking struggle to attract me and ask me out was well rewarded. I, too, felt happy to have such a sweet guy. Whenever he saw an Indian with a Chinese woman, he would point it out, saying that we, too, are like them. I got to know more about his affectionate and trustworthy side, and felt secure that he would be mine for a long time.

Notes

1. Pseudonym.
2. All names in this story are pseudonyms.
3. Pseudonym.

CHAPTER TWELVE

~

The Romance of Library Conferences

Library conferences are well known for their networking potential. The social aspects of a conference are often what define the success of the conference. Much work can be achieved in a networking atmosphere in a profession where we are programmed to seek and give information. The same potential exists in committees. It's only logical that a meeting of a community of shared values is likely to create some romantic sparks as well.

Paul's Story

My wife and I met at a library conference held in Providence, Rhode Island, in April 1998. At the time I was living and working in a library in South Florida, and she was doing the same in Alberta. We ended up attending the same social event on the first night of the conference, and spent the evening talking about many things including, of course, favorite books.

While we enjoyed each other's company, we never thought anything would come of it, what with us living so many thousands of miles away. A few weeks after the conference though, I sent her a copy of one of the books we discussed, and an e-mail pen pal relationship ensued.

This e-mail correspondence allowed us to get to know one another professionally and personally, and we made arrangements to see each other in person again that fall while I was teaching one weekend only a short flight from where she lived. From then on we were able to meet about every three months at library conferences or on vacation until I was able to move to Canada a year later in November of 1999.

We were married in June of 2001 and now have two little bookworms of our own.

Dawna's[1] Story

How do two librarians from opposite ends of the country meet and fall in love? At a library conference, of course! I'm originally from the east coast of Canada and was near the end of a year-long contract in Alberta when I attended the Library Association of Alberta (LAA) conference at the Jasper Park Lodge. That weekend I saw the Rockies for the first time and met a librarian from Saskatchewan. Although I had always intended to return to the Maritimes after my western adventure, the combination of spectacular outdoor scenery and a new romance compelled me to stay in Alberta.

We celebrated our first anniversary together at the conference the following year and later that summer we were engaged. A few months after attending our third LAA conference together we were married. Librarians in attendance included: our master of ceremonies, two members of our bridal parties, our guitarist, and several of our guests.

Elizabeth's[2] Story

Is it really over between us? My soul cries no. We met at a national library conference that my home city hosted more than ten or eleven years ago. When he walked across the room at that opening reception, he took my breath away. There was an instant connection, though unacknowledged, since we very quickly established I was married. The following year, on the other side of the country, his city hosted the conference. That attraction was still there. I left for another area of librarianship and to other conferences so our paths stopped crossing. Returning to our specialty (and conference), there he was again.

More years, more conferences. We'd chat, sit together at sessions—all very innocent and collegial, except for that smoldering heat.

Another year, another conference. Then, one year, walking back to the hotel after lunch together, he broached the subject we avoided all those years. That last night of the conference, we surprised ourselves with the intensity of our unleashed emotions. In spite of the impossibility of our situation—our geographic distance, my marriage, and his relationship—we stumbled into love. What I half feared would happen inevitably did. I lost my heart to him and left my comfortable life with my husband. And he broke up with his girlfriend.

We started seeing each other outside of conferences and even (quietly) affirmed that we were a couple at them. But we still lived a million miles apart. Over time, our joy and happiness when we were together made the loneliness and yearning during our times apart unendurable. But our love and passion has not faded. We're destined to lodge in each other's heart. Our song? In memory of the last night of our impossible, unforgettable romance, Chip Taylor and Carrie Rodriguez's version of "Angel of the Morning."

As a postscript, I was at a library conference the other week, a regional one that he never attended. God help me; I was unprepared for the pain of his absence.

David and Elise's Story

We met at the sixth Northern Exposure to Leadership Conference in February of 2002 in the Canadian Rockies. One of the nice things about the Emerald Lake Lodge was the hot tub, so after the day's events were over, a few of us would head to the hot tub to relax. That's where Elise and I spent a lot of talking and getting to know one another. Later a friendship formed which blossomed into a romance. We are now married.

Nancy's Story

My husband, Mike, and I worked for neighboring county library systems in Maryland and had attended four previous state and national conferences but had never met until that fateful night at the May 1996 Maryland Library Association Conference in Hagerstown. We didn't meet at one of the programs but at one of the evening's entertainments, country and western line dancing, led by my colleague and friend, Sandy Owen. I was one of her spotters. This cowboy (who hadn't planned to stay overnight at the conference, but had a colleague who needed a roommate) next to me with the boots and hat (Mike is from Dallas after all) appeared to have two left feet (he's actually an excellent dancer) and was asking for help. We were talking and dancing away until my friend sent me down to the other end of the line to help some people. Afterward, Mike and I managed to continue our conversation and we've literally been together ever since. We met in May, got engaged July 4, and married on December 21, 1996—a different sort of "May/December" relationship. (Although Mike is eighteen years older than me. His first career was in the foreign service.) Three states (North Carolina, South Carolina, and now New Jersey) of library service later we are still librarians very much in love.

Tanja's Story

I met my husband on a university librarian search committee. We had been without a university librarian for more than a year and he had just arrived to the university as an assistant to the vice president academic. As the vice president was acting university librarian my husband was asked to join the committee. He says that he spent more time in the library during our university librarian search than he did completing his two degrees.

Sarah's Story

My husband, Steve, and I met in the Pace University Mortola Library in the spring of 2001. In a strange twist, Steve was interviewing for the position which was vacated by my sister, who had met a man online and had moved from New York to Nebraska to be with him. Steve had a successful interview, and answered my all-important "Mets or Yankees?" question correctly—Mets! We became fast friends, and on July 4, 2001, while watching fireworks, Steve held my hand.

We were married on October 26, 2003, and we both continue to work for the Pace University Library. Library couples abound: one of

Steve's mentors is also married to a school librarian. And we recently attended the wedding of two friends who are both librarians!

Nina's[3] Story

In 1984 I was working in a public library in my village in the Netherlands. I was married and had three little children. We invited several applicants for an interview. One of them was a man, also married with three children, and I felt myself immediately attracted to him. This man got the job (it wasn't just my decision) and we became colleagues and friends. We went to the beach with our two families and those kinds of things. He and my husband became friends.

After eighteen months this man (my boss) and I became lovers. Though it was very special it was also a very sad moment, because we both had partners and children. I had to leave the library; we could no longer work together within our team. I also started library education at that time and was going to work in a bigger public library.

We both divorced. First we lived separately in two houses, because there was a lot going on. We both had children and we both had shared custody with our ex-partners and there was also a lot of grief. But we were still lovers.

After eighteen months we decided to live in one house (his house), where we lived as a family with our six children as follows: one week with my children, one week with all the children, one week with his children and one week without children, just the two of us, and then again the same pattern. We still had our jobs and I had my study, so you can imagine it was a very heavy time and there were also a lot of problems.

Many people asked us later how we could manage that. But we survived and in 1994 we married. Our children are grown up now and have their own lives. The eldest daughter is even married herself now.

We are still very happy. We are still working in a public library (not the same one any more). So a library isn't dull at all!

The music that was special from that time is Prince (we went together to his concert in Utrecht, a town in the Netherlands), The Style Council with Paul Webber, Everything But The Girl (a group), Matt Bianco, and The Scorpions ("Still Loving You").

But we also had our sad moments. During those times I listened to Level 42 (a very sad song: I forget the title, but I still know the melody) and my husband listened to Peter Gabriel and Kate Bush ("Don't Give Up"). This is my story with a happy ending.

Christoph's Story

It happened on Wednesday, August 6, 2003, at the reception of the Austrian Embassy on the occasion of the 69th IFLA General Conference and Council in Berlin; it was where I met Anne, my wife, for the first time.

The story begins in 1997–1998 when I worked at the German Libraries Institute and was involved in the successful application of the German Libraries Association and the City of Berlin to hold the 69th IFLA General Conference in 2003 in Berlin. And it continued in 2000 when I became conference coordinator in the Berlin Secretariat for the organization of this conference. However, when the conference started on August 1, 2003, my work was not yet done. Particularly in the first conference days my head was full of all those tiny things that had to be organized and to be cared for, so that I was unable to think of anything else.

That is, until this unforgettable Wednesday evening in the conference week, when traditionally foreign delegates were invited by their embassies to a reception. The German-speaking delegates were invited by the Austrian embassy and since I arrived a little late, the buffet offered almost nothing but small hot sausages and an even much stronger horseradish. I don't remember if it was because of the hot sausages, the very strong horseradish, the extraordinary heat on that day, or simply the good feeling of having reached the halfway point of the conference, that I drank a cool beer with some colleagues I knew. And suddenly Anne stood right beside me. We didn't know each other but I got into conversation with her easily. At this time, Anne had just finished her study of library science at the Humboldt University of Berlin and had begun to write her thesis with the topic "Promotion of Reading." After the reception we couldn't decide whether to go home so we went for a short stroll to a pub nearby at the Potsdamer Platz. Since then we have been a couple.

After the conference we visited each other in Berlin and Dresden (where Anne lived) until she moved into my Berlin flat at the beginning of 2004. It was then again in a library setting on January 9 that I asked Anne, during the opening of an exhibition at the Berlin State Library, if she was willing to marry me. We got married in Berlin on August 6, 2004, the exact day one year after we got to know each other for the first time. And it will not be surprising if I tell you that our honeymoon was a library study tour to Paris, France, organized by the Berufsverband Information und Bibliothek (BIB) in September 2004.

Notes

1. Pseudonym.
2. Pseudonym.
3. Pseudonym.

CHAPTER THIRTEEN

~

Romance with an International Twist

Rachelle's[1] Story

Rachelle was on sabbatical in another country, spending the year as a visiting scholar at a library school. Tom[2] was a local library director. They met one day when he came to the school to give a guest lecture. Their eyes met several times during the hour, and afterward he invited her to visit his library. So began a romance that lasted well past Rachelle's sabbatical year.

Rachelle was living in a graduate student residence. She had soon realized that she was too accustomed to comfort to live in a dorm with shared bathrooms, but the location was convenient and the fees reasonable. Toward the end of her stay, she was offered the opportunity to be the senior residence don. With the title came a large beautiful en suite room with a sunny bay window. During the weeks she was there, it seemed as though the sun shone on that room every day. She and Tom got into a routine. He would come to the residence when he left his office for the day, bringing strawberries and fresh farm cream or some other sensuous treat. They would draw the drapes, put music on the cassette player (usually 10cc—this was the 1980s), and enjoy the next few hours in each other's company.

Although the romance is now a thing of the past, Rachelle and Tom have remained friends. They usually arrange to meet if they happen to find themselves in the same country at the same time. Tom will talk for a while about his grandchildren or his latest travels, but eventually he'll say, "Remember those wonderful strawberries we had?" and they will smile at each other and enjoy the memories.

Marion's Story

My story dates back to the 1960s. I was secretary of the African Studies Association libraries and librarian of the African studies program of Boston University. In May 1963 we held a meeting at the Library of Congress and I was reporting on the acquisition and handling of government documents from the African countries. Attending from the Library of Congress was a new employee named Roderick Macdonald. We went out to dinner that night and were married in January 1964. He finished his Ph.D. at Edinburgh University with field work in Malawi, East Africa, where I worked on setting up the new university library at the University of Malawi.

Catharine's Story

I am a librarian and was working in the library at Thunderbird, the Garvin School of International Management in Phoenix, Arizona, when I met someone special. Oscar was a Mexican graduate student visiting Thunderbird for a ten-day orientation for his distance education–based master's program. It was my job to give the library instruction session to the hundred and twenty Mexican students. I remember seeing Oscar in the session (he now says that he asked questions just to get noticed). During the next ten days he made frequent visits to the library and did little to hide his interest.

Oscar recalls that at the closing party, there was a line of Mexican men waiting to dance with the American librarian (I didn't see it!) but he pushed them aside reminding them that they were married!

He insisted that I accompany the group on a trip on the last day to the Grand Canyon. Though I was very tired after staying up all night with the Latin revelers I went, and Oscar and I spent ten hours that day on a bus talking and getting to know each other better.

Back at Thunderbird, we shared our first kiss in the library parking lot and said good-bye. I figured that I now had a good friend in Mexico, but didn't expect much more.

Thank goodness for technology, however. Once Oscar was home, the e-mails began to arrive and we would chat regularly. The song that reminds me most of that time is Andrea Bocelli's "Volaré" since Oscar once sent me a digital postcard that played that song.

Two years later, we danced to that song at our wedding. Today, we live in Monterrey, Mexico where I work half time as a librarian at the Virtual University at Monterrey Technical University, and spend the rest of my time raising our two boys, Diego and Luke.

Joan's Story

Cliff and I met while I was business librarian at the headquarters of a large international corporation in the United States. It was 1978 and we first met each other at a departmental meeting. Cliff had just returned from a job in Indonesia and he was to become the manager of management information (the library was part of that department). My boss was out sick and she asked that I go up to him and invite him to tour the library to let him know we were ready to support his group. I did, and he was impressed. We again spoke at a company picnic—he remembers the visor I wore with an emblem of a tennis racquet and a golf club. He loves playing golf and tennis—and so did I.

A few months later he asked me out, and I couldn't believe a *manager* was asking me out! I've always told my friends *never* date anyone you work with! Also, I was paranoid about people finding out we were "dating" as I didn't want to jeopardize our jobs. So, we'd meet outside, or down the street. One of Cliff's coworkers found out about me, knew I was Italian, and started to nickname me "Sofia," after Sophia Loren. Little did I know that name would come in handy fifteen years later!

We had a great time and fell in love. After an ALA or SLA conference I gave him a sticker: "Novel lover!" Then, there was a hiatus. No dating . . . and I didn't know why. It turned out that I was going to report directly to him—as I had worked my way up from cataloger/reference librarian, to reference department head, to chief librarian. That was my dream in library school: to become head of a corporate library. My old boss left, there was some shuffling, and Cliff became my direct boss. I guess he was hesitant as to how we would relate. It was hard to concentrate sometimes! He was handsome and wonderful. But we did fine. We were always professional on the job.

Then Cliff received notice that he was to be transferred to Toronto, Canada—in two months. We were both shocked. (International companies need to move their people quickly to where the jobs are!) So, in August, we decided to talk at Christmas to see how we were handling a long-distance romance. I didn't see how it would turn out well.

The week after he left I was very sad. Everything around me (inside the library and out) reminded me of Cliff. The Friday after he left, I was invited to a company party but my heart wasn't happy so I stayed home. I got a call that evening. It was Cliff on the phone, and he proposed!

We married the following May and have lived in South America (Colombia and Chile) and Australia, and have visited Antarctica, Fiji, Taiwan, and Greece. We have two children.

We moved to Chile with the children in 1993. Knowing that Latinos have a hard time pronouncing the letter "j" I decided to change my name. My middle name is Marie—but there are hundreds of Marias in Latin America, so I chose "Sofia." It worked like a dream.

So you can meet a prince via the library!

Egil and Lucia's[3] Story

Our story sounds very special to us, and, we still wonder how it was possible that Egil and I met in such an unusual place and circumstances. We have to take a little step backward and explain why a Norwegian librarian and an Italian library assistant happened to be in Aberystwyth, Wales, at the same time.

Egil:
I had lived in Trondheim, Norway, almost all my life, apart from four years in Oslo in the mid-1980s when I was studying to become a qualified librarian. During the 1990s I was studying music and working in libraries in Trondheim, most of the time in the local university library. Apart from some holiday trips abroad as a child, and a couple of trips to Berlin and London, I have never traveled much, partly because of

interest, but mostly because of money, wanting to use it for my other interests.

In 2000 my employer offered me the chance to go to a conference in Latvia about interlibrary loans, an offer I declined after some consideration; the place looked quite interesting, but I didn't find much that interested me in the conference program. Later the same year, there was a general encouragement on our university library intranet to have a look at the program of a summer school in Wales and flag any interest in attending. I read this and found some time to look at the program, which looked both relevant to my job and very interesting. I applied for funding to go there during early spring 2001, and my employer agreed to send me. Fortunately for me, a colleague who had seniority, and who had thought seriously about going, decided not to apply.

Apart from hoping to get a lot of inspiring input to bring back to my workplace, the course and going abroad also offered me the possibility of immersing myself in something interesting to take my thoughts off other matters, as a relationship I was hoping to continue ended just a couple of months before the course started.

Lucia:
I, on the other hand, was almost new to the library world. I had always lived in Milan, where my course of studies and my work activities had been a little meandering: I had graduated in arts and humanities, but had only found a job in IT after attending a one-year course to become a programmer. I worked in IT for fourteen years, but after a sad period during and following the illness and death of my beloved mother, I thought I couldn't stand the cold and inhumane IT setting any more (in spite of having very good colleagues), and I decided I wanted to work in a library instead.

I studied librarianship hard enough to win a public competition, and I started working in the University Library of Milan. I enjoyed my job very much, but after two years I thought that an in-depth course focused on electronic services could be a good chance to widen my knowledge and skills. So I decided to invest my savings in the International Graduate Summer School in Library and Information Science held at the University of Wales, Aberystwyth. Also, I had always liked traveling and being abroad, and, although a little scared by the fact that my knowledge of English was far from perfect, I was nonetheless very excited at the idea of meeting colleagues from other countries and taking part in the course.

There was also one more reason to be glad to leave for a while: my firm intention of being single had just been unexpectedly badly shaken, and I had just experienced a bitter disappointment in my emotional life; one more reason to go away for a while and try to forget.

Egil and Lucia:

The course started in the second half of June 2001, and was divided into two parts, each lasting two weeks. The delegates registered with the first part were only seven: from Iceland, Italy, Indonesia, Uganda, the United States, and two from Norway. There were interesting lessons morning and afternoon, held by friendly professors, all very well informed on the most recent progress and problems of electronic services in libraries. There was a lot of time to exchange experiences during the lessons and share our company, even with tutors, at meals and breaks. After two weeks a few delegates left, and a few new ones from other parts of Europe and Asia joined us.

The first two weeks the two of us talked together now and then, but during the second half of the course we spent an increasing amount of time in the evenings in the common room, talking of past and present. Little by little Lucia discovered the good qualities in Egil, and how pleasant it was to be in his company. Egil on his side found Lucia to be intelligent, beautiful, humorous, and in general a pleasure to be with, and as such a welcome counterpoint to himself.

By the end of the course, we admitted that we would have missed each other a lot and that something had happened in our hearts that could never be described. Quite unlike his normal behavior, Egil realized that a quick decision had to be made, and the very last evening he proposed to Lucia. Lucia very happily accepted.

We left Aberystwyth the following morning, with the rest of the group. When we finally parted in London, Egil offered to visit Lucia in Italy the same summer. And since visiting each other wasn't easy, nor could it happen very often (for work and economic reasons), and we were already quite sure that we wanted to spend the rest of our lives together, we decided to marry as soon as possible, and to move somewhere where both could find work, understand the language, and be within easy reach of our families in Italy and Norway.

So when Egil found a job in London, Lucia organized the wedding in Milan. We got married on April 5, 2002, and we both work in London now, in two different libraries.

We love each other more every day, and we still wonder at the incredible series of events that had to happen so that we could meet. Even today we smile thinking, "If I had gone to the other congress, . . ." "If I had worked in IT one more year, . . ." and all the other "ifs" that could have made things different and would never have allowed us to meet at exactly that stage of our lives. And we are quite confident that the divine hand that has so wisely and providentially lead our lives until now will never abandon us.

Notes

1. Pseudonym.
2. Pseudonym.
3. Pseudonyms.

CHAPTER FOURTEEN

Multiple Copies

A number of stories suggested that finding romance in a library is a pattern in some people's lives. Sometimes the pattern is even repeated through several generations. On occasion a divorce doesn't deter someone from finding another romantic partner in a library. The ex-husband of a college librarian I know moved across the country to work in another college. He promptly fell in love with another librarian who held a position similar to his ex-wife's. Perhaps the pattern is caused by a romance with the library world itself.

Steph's Story

I have not only found love in a library, I've found it twice. I am a student, and I work at my university library. The first time I found love was with a coworker. We bonded over shelving, of all things. We used to run away to kiss in the stacks. It was fun and gave us a little dorky thrill. But, alas, it did not last. However, I have now found a new library romance. One moment I was discussing a loan query with him, the next I found myself falling in love. It's going swimmingly.

Lisa's Story

I met my husband when we were both doing our last year of work experience in our respective courses, he in engineering and me in librarianship. We worked for an engineering company and virtually shared the same desk. It wasn't love at first sight as I was going out with someone else. That romance ended when the person I was seeing was deported after having stayed beyond his student visa. Strangely enough, I met him at the university library!

My husband and I have now been married for over eight years and we have been together since 1993. I've been lucky in love in libraries.

Marietta's Story

I met both my husbands in a library setting. My first husband, Peter, tall, blond, and handsome, proposed to me on bended knee in the Scarborough College Library, in the beautiful surroundings of the Scarborough College Campus. The campus had been built in the 1960s and was located in the idyllic setting of the Rouge Valley in Ontario. I was a nineteen-year-old undergraduate and fresh as the college was new. I, like the books which surrounded me with their uncracked spines, was approaching love in the spirit of newness. I had just completed my first semester of my first year at college when the proposal came.

Peter and I married after a year of dating—mainly in the library. It was a romantic proposal in a small lounge area off the main library corridor. We got married because at the time the morals were such that we could not live together. He was a year my senior.

I did realize though that there was more to libraries than studying, but I hadn't yet decided to become a librarian. The marriage lasted only until I graduated from my master's program at the University of Toronto's Faculty of Library Science. Now my time would be spent in the library. My love transferred from Peter to the books inside the college library—my real passion.

Twenty years later, I met my present husband, Matthias, at the Toronto Reference Library. He was writing a script. He usually chose to work there on the fifth floor in the Sir Arthur Conan Doyle Room where I worked as a librarian in the languages and literature department. He watched me and followed me one day as I went to the coffee shop across the road for a quick caffeine fix. He spoke to me in line as I was standing there in my fur coat with my then long, flowing blonde hair. I replied that I really needed a cup of coffee. We smiled at each other—just a casual encounter in the big city. Little did I realize he had been watching me and saw me as the proud lioness, as inspiration of a poem he was later to pen.

When he saw me again leaving the library he asked me out to lunch at the nearby falafel restaurant. The waiter asked whether he would like some hot sauce. He replied that he liked his food mild and his women spicy.

He spent many hours at the library while he was writing a script. He shared with me his love of Sir Arthur Conan Doyle, and the libraries he had visited worldwide. Ahh . . . the Toronto Reference Library does draw some interesting characters into its midst and not all of them are homeless.

We have been happily married for over eleven years and have a beautiful daughter.

Sarah's[1] Story

Both my marriages are library connected. My first husband was the treasurer of the library board, a recent widower, when I moved to his town. A gracious gentleman, he would at first offer me a ride home from the library at lunch. When he discovered how much I loved to drive, I did the driving. I think it was at first about two lonely people who loved books. He was much older than I was but eventually we married and had eight months and two weeks together before his devastating death. But the self-assurance he gave me stayed with me all my life.

In the second case, I was trying to get a regional library up and running and experiencing frustrating delays at every turn. I discovered the cause of the delays but could do nothing about it. However the news editor of the local paper sent a reporter to enquire about the delay. The reporter asked pointed questions and I sent him to the chair of the board. But I ascertained who the news editor was.

Some months later friends invited me to join them for a weekend in the country. When I heard that my nemesis would be there I decided to accompany them and find out what this ogre was actually like. We had only just arrived in a bitterly cold cabin when the editor and his son turned up. It turned out that he too was a recent widower.

Before too long his older and younger daughters appeared and when I saw his blonde six-year-old, reason went out the window. We danced the next night and his son decided I would be a good choice and kept pouring me drinks of the cognac his father had imported. So, I gave him my phone number and then spent forty-three years with the ogre.

His son is now a retired professor; his older daughter a nurse; the young blonde daughter is still blonde but not as naturally as previously and working for the federal government. We have grandchildren and even six great-grandchildren. But I do not let him forget his first assault on my library position.

Damon's Story

I met my wife in the summer of 1966 at Princeton Theological Seminary. I was beginning my second year and she, her first. I was working in the library that summer, and she was taking an immersion course in biblical Greek before the semester began. In what was then almost entirely all-male Princeton, any young woman stood out in a crowd. As I headed to work, I spotted her on her first day of class, the only female among a bunch of guys waiting for the library (where her class was held) to open. The next morning I introduced myself and asked her out. One thing led to another, and we were married at the end of that school year.

It seems almost inevitable that my wife and I would have met around a library. My mother and father did too. She was a student assistant in charge of a science branch library at Rice University in the 1920s, and he was a struggling engineering student whom she met and tutored there. Ironically, our daughter met her husband at the same university, where both of them were librarians in the 1990s.

Chris's Story

In the 1950s, 1960s, and 1970s, UK public libraries were labor intensive, with large teams of junior assistants serving huge banks—twenty feet long in our case—of Brown issue (cards and wallets, if you've never seen the Brown issue system). I worked for a year at Walthamstow Central Library (about six miles from the city of London), where we had a team of twelve junior assistants, five men and seven women, all aged seventeen to twenty-five, plus five senior assistants, only two of whom were over forty. The results were pretty inevitable! I met my wife there, and found later that the chief librarian (born 1922) had done exactly the same in the early 1950s. We are now neighbors, with eighty-five years of marriage between us. There were several other couples from the same basis, too.

My wife and I married on a Wednesday, the library's closing day, so our friends could be present, instead of the more usual Saturday.

Romance in the Library—Nancy E. Black

When you are a person who decides at the age of seven to become a librarian, and when you are a person who starts working in a library as a page at the age of twelve earning ninety cents an hour, and when you tend to think of yourself as a librarian almost before anything else and view the librarian profession with energy, commitment, and passion, it follows logically that a great deal of your life, including romance and love, will revolve around the library. But, the partner of such a person must understand the significance and the power of the library within the being of this person, because sometimes in a relationship such as this, the library will come first and the love will come second. And some people have a difficult time understanding that, including the librarian herself.

When I think back, most of my romances either began in the library, or had a strong library connection. I met my first real boyfriend in Quebec City when I was sixteen. A number of high schools visited the city during the Winter Carnival Bonhomme festival and somehow or other I met a boy from another school and we spent a lot of time innocently talking, walking, and getting to know one another. He was the first boy I had held hands with, the first boy who put his arm around me, and the first boy who hugged me. I don't recall now if we kissed or not. For some reason we didn't exchange addresses or phone numbers when the trip was completed, we simply said our good-byes. This boy, however, was smart and he figured out how to track me down; now that I think about it, he might have made a good librarian.

He knew that I worked in public library as a page and he sent a letter to the chief librarian explaining how he knew me and asked if his letter could be passed on to me. Unfortunately, the administration took the responsibility of guarding my virtue very seriously and didn't pass the letter on. Nothing daunted, this boy, working on very few clues, managed to figure out which high school I was likely to attend and sent another letter off, only this time, being addressed to me, it was passed directly to me. For the next few years, we shared an intense writing friendship, but without being able to visit each other, the friendship faded away. Sometimes I still wonder what happened to that young man.

I met my next boyfriend when I was eighteen, in grade thirteen, and still working as a page at my local public library; he was a college boy and was a few years older than me, much to the discomfort of my parents. He came into the library one evening and asked me for help. I showed him the area he needed and then directed him to the reference staff for further help (it was always impressed upon us pages that we "were not supposed to help the patrons" and so I was a little daring when I helped him). I thought nothing of the exchange, but a few nights later, he called the library and asked to speak to me. He must have described me, because I don't believe I gave him a name. He asked me out for a date and I accepted. We saw each other for several months, but when I began university, my horizons broadened significantly and I soon ended the relationship.

University was wonderful for me: I blossomed from ugly duckling wallflower to confident social butterfly. I met another young man, not in the library, but in drama class, who was to be my first really serious "I am in love" boyfriend. I worked part time in the university library shelving books and he used to come in during my shifts, find me, steal passionate kisses in the stacks, and then make dates with me for later. Our code language of love had its roots in books and reading: "studying," "curling up with a good book," "between the covers of a good book," "reading a good book." That summer that boy, some of our friends, and I had summer jobs with a public library system which were to travel to various branches performing children's plays scripted from children's picture books that I had selected.

When I finished my undergrad and went off to do my MLS, that boy followed me, because he loved me and I loved him. While I attended library school, he worked in the theater, but in his free time, he always knew where to find me in the library so we could share passionate kisses and make dates for later.

I loved library school, but sometimes it brings about changes in people that aren't anticipated and so it was with me. I found that I looked at that boy through different eyes and even though he loved me still and I loved him, I wasn't so sure anymore that he was "the one"; and so after six years of fun, laughter, passion, love, and all those stolen kisses in the stacks, that relationship ended. How is it that something as powerful as love can also be so fragile and easily shattered? From time to time I wonder about that boy, where he is now, and what might have been. Sometimes, after I've recalled some memory, he comes to me in my dreams, holds me, caresses me, kisses me, and the passion I remember so well returns briefly. And in the morning, I am left with the bittersweet memory of that boy and the love we shared.

I was working at yet another library system when I met the man who was to become my husband. I had hired a touring theater company to perform a show for young adult audiences throughout the library system. When the actors arrived to set up, I met them, made sure they had everything they needed for the performance and chatted again with them after the show. Of the group, there was one individual I noticed who had a quiet and pleasant manner.

On various occasions after that performance, I kept running into that particular person either on the street, or a coffee shop, or at various improvisation performances (he was a member of a local improvisation group). Each time we enjoyed a brief conversation. I'm not sure now how many times these meetings occurred, but one day when I was sitting at my desk, he dropped into the library to say hello. He had just come from an office supply store and, confessing his weakness for such stores, proceeded to show me his purchases. We talked and then, not wanting to take up more of my time, he left. As I watched him leave I thought to myself: this guy didn't just come in here to show me his pencils, erasers, and staple remover, I think he likes me and I'm going to call him up and ask him out. And so I did. That I took the initiative with that phone call, upon reflection, seems to have set the tone for our relationship: I was the one who suggested we marry, I was the one who decided when it was time to conceive (both times), and I have been the one whose career has taken us from pillar to post around the country. In short, I seem to be "wearing the pants"—an expression I absolutely hate—but there you are. And yes, sadly, there are many times when the library comes first and the love second. But, when I need a sounding board, a friend, wisdom, or strength, he is there for me, he is my anchor and I could not imagine my life without him.

Note

1. Pseudonym.

CHAPTER FIFTEEN

Library Cupids

A number of stories I received involved a third party, in some way connected to a library, who brought the romantic couple together.

Susan's Story

My husband and I met when we were both clerks at the main public library in Austin. I was working part time while I was finishing library school, and we both remember when we first met at work. We became fast friends and when I finished library school before most of my friends, we began to hang out more and more. Then I quit my job to take a trip to Europe, and when I got back, we kept hanging out until he finally kissed me. We've been together ever since, and we even had our boss from the library as our guest book attendant at our wedding— since he hired both of us, he technically introduced us!

Sally's Story

My husband and I met in the library at the University of Cape Town in South Africa. He had come to visit an old friend with whom I worked, in the cataloging department on the top floor of the library building. My friend was quite taken aback when he walked right into the department as the head was quite a formidable lady; so my friend told him to go downstairs and meet her at the catalog (we still had a card catalog in those days!). I had to check something in the catalog and was somewhat intrigued, so I went down a little bit later, and she called me over to introduce me. Our mutual friend whispered to him, "She's a nice girl, take her out," so he did. Much later we ended up marrying and subsequently moved to Canada with our baby. We had another child in Canada.

Monika's Story

Libraries have been one of the best things in my life and have run through every part of it. As a little girl I loved going to the public library in town and was fascinated by the long red fingernails of the librarian sorting the issue card holders. At home we also had no comics or magazines and I loved reading those that were available in the library. Whereas my primary school (a private school) had classroom libraries and very interesting (imported) textbooks, my high school library was rather pathetic and very little used. I would dream of one day making it to the big time, when I would come back to this library with a whole truck full of lovely new books for teenagers.

After leaving school in the 1970s I studied library science part time in Pretoria, South Africa, and had a colleague who worked in the local research library. She and I attended the same classes at the University of Pretoria's extramural campus.

During one long weekend my parents invited my friend to accompany us on a camping/hiking expedition in the Drakensberg Mountains. In the evening we were sitting around the campfire and got to discussing political issues. My friend and I were defending opposing viewpoints and had quite a heated debate, but went to sleep quite amicably all the same. Just before dropping off I heard her mutter something to the effect that I held opinions very similar to those of "that guy at work" and that she really thought she should introduce us to one another—which she duly did on a blind date a few weeks later. He was a librarian who later became a professor in library science and who had a great interest in professional research.

My friend (and half of the research library) attended our wedding and she was always very proud of having been our fairy godmother/matchmaker. We still keep in touch.

My husband was recruited by a visionary and principal of what was then the new University of Bophuthatswana (now South Africa, North West Province). He started the first library at this institution from scratch in one bedroom of a staff dwelling and with only one telephone line to the outside world. At one stage there was great happiness as we were informed that the bookshelves had at last arrived by train. We rushed off to collect them only to find that the suppliers hadn't included a single screw!

My husband had gone to Mmabatho (capital of Bophuthatswana) first and I followed after a month with two little sons. The reticulation on our house hadn't been completed so we would drive off through the veldt to the house in which the library was located and all take our daily baths before going back to our supper.

I imagine that I shall still be enjoying libraries in my old age when I hope I'll have more time to read.

Bill's Story

We first met at the Nova Scotia Community College in the spring of 1999. I had just started the library and information technician program where Denise was well into her second year.

Oddly enough, on the orientation day in the main classroom, our first impressions didn't bode well: I thought she was some sort of control freak whereas she found me to be moody (little did she know that I was working three jobs and had only had two hours of sleep in a plow truck in the parking lot!).

Because of this first impression, we kept our distance. But we did have a mutual friend, who was in my class, by the name of Jen. Jen and I became close friends and eventually started the beginnings of a small practical joke tit-for-tat war. This comes into play later. Meanwhile, Denise had graduated in April of 1999 and immediately found a circulation job at a local university and was still not interested in me.

One day, Jen's refrigerator stopped working. I had found a cheap used one and was going to deliver it. Denise had agreed to help. It was at this point that Denise became curious in me. I'm still not sure how I warranted it! In a dubious use of the library consortium files, Denise found out my address and phone number and heard from Jen that I was also working part time in the Community College Library. She decided to contact me for coffee.

When Denise started to ask me about coffee, I assumed, in my para-noia, that Jen was setting up some sort of elaborate practical joke. I decided to go along with it though, as my own curiosity had taken hold. I wanted to see how devious Jen could be!

The night went well enough, including an intense discussion on how people are mostly sheep, and ended very nicely. And when nothing else had occurred, I suspected that my first assumption might be wrong. Many other dates occurred and we ended up living together by that spring. And even though we can never agree if our coffee was a first date or a pre-date requisite, it was definitely the first of our time together.

Beware the Patron Bearing Gifts—Maureen[1]

When I returned from a meeting one afternoon I was greeted by a coworker who said conspiratorially, "An admirer of yours stopped by earlier." This coworker was notorious for pointing out eligible-looking young men (and not-so-eligible men, too, since once she directed me toward a priest so handsome we all started calling him "Father What-A-Waste"). Then she'd send me over to see if they needed any help, so I was fairly dubious about this admirer thing.

But she said, "A nice young man came in about an hour ago asking for you. I told him you were at a meeting, but I'd be happy to give you a message. He said, 'Actually, we haven't exactly met. She's just placed holds for me a few times.' I offered to place a hold for him, but he said, 'I was actually going to ask her out on a date.' So I told him exactly when you'd be back (so much for privacy!) and he said he would come back this evening."

Hmm, I thought. I asked her for more details. What did he look like? Did he leave his name? Most importantly, what exactly had I placed on hold for him? She gave me the thumbnail sketch of his appearance—sounded promising enough—and told me his name, which didn't ring a bell. She had no idea what holds I placed for him. Needless to say, I was useless for the rest of the afternoon, wondering who in the world had been asking about me and if, in fact, he would come back.

About five-thirty that evening, I was sitting at the reference desk when I noticed a slight, dark-haired young man in a sweatshirt and baseball cap coming down the stairs with a red rose in his hand. As soon as I saw him, I remembered! Not his name, but his many requests for obscure foreign science fiction videos. After a few feverish and hushed minutes of brief acquaintance-making at the reference desk, we agreed to meet for coffee after I got off work.

A strange and frenetic two months ensued. This young man gave me more gifts, oftentimes books and almost always in public, at which point he would drop to his knees to present them to me. Not having a job, he spent an inordinate amount of time mooning over me at the reference desk. Mooning and knee-dropping seem like fantasy expressions of appropriate adoration . . . unless you're trying to maintain even a modicum of professionalism.

During our mercifully brief relationship, I compiled about fourteen thousand reasons why I should never have gone on a date with this man in the first place (pushing thirty and still living with parents; still sleeping with stuffed sheep; still thinks he's going to be a blues guitarist when he grows up; can't possibly get a real job because of possible interference with loftier career goals). One does well not to date patrons in general (mainly, because coworkers take an unhealthy interest in all lurid facets of the relationship, which does not come in so handy in later years when the same people are now one's employees who take smug pleasure in reminding one of a not-so-dignified courtship).

Since then, I've made it a point of making sure the men I date aren't registered library users. It just makes everything a whole lot simpler.

Deanna's Story

I didn't meet my boyfriend at the library; I did meet his sister there though. Monica and I both work for the same library system and would occasionally bump into one another at various branches. One day, when we were getting off work, she asked me what I was looking for in a man and would I mind being set up. I said that he would have to be Christian, single, and straight and that I wouldn't mind being set up at all. She then asked whether looks or a sense of humor were more important (this was her brother after all). I answered "sense of humor," and she gave me and Peter each other's phone number. We later met at the local Chapters. We had agreed to meet an hour before the movie we were going to see. He was late, very late, but we started talking and four hours later we realized we had missed the movie. Though we've had a few periods of angst, doubt, and negotiation we are still together and now talking engagement.

Judith's Story

My husband and I met because of a library. In the fall of 1982, I was working in the agricultural economics reference room at the University of Illinois at Urbana-Champaign. A friend (my future sister-in-law) worked in the same building and had been talking about her big brother Steve.

One day she said that he had a question that she thought I could help him with and that he would be in town that weekend for her birthday (he lived in Springfield, ninety miles away). I arranged to meet him on Sunday at my office. It turned out that the answer to his question was at the State Library in Springfield, but he took me out for hot chocolate anyway. I figured that was the end of that. Little did I know.

A couple of days later, I got a call from him to the effect that he knew that my birthday was this weekend and how would I like to go out to a movie to celebrate it (his sister told him my birthday was just a week after hers). "But you live in Springfield," I said.

"No problem," said he. He drove over, we went to see *ET* (in its first release), and again I thought that was that. (I am a slow learner.)

He drove over (or I drove to Springfield) every weekend until January. He came to my parents' house for Thanksgiving; I went to his for Christmas, when he gave me his high school ring. On our third date (to see Barry Manilow) he started saying, "When we get married. . . ." Having been married and divorced I responded, "Been there, done that, didn't like it, not going to do it again." As would become his common response, he ignored me.

While I was in Champaign and he in Springfield, we both worked for professors and had access to the University of Illinois's computers.

So, we used its message system to talk to each other. You could say that we courted by e-mail.

I didn't think about him seriously until I was on my graduation-from-library-school present from my parents—a trip to Yucatan, Mexico. Since I didn't see him for a couple of weekends, I discovered I missed him. He gave me his fraternity pin for Valentine's Day. When I came out to Ohio to look for a place to live (I had accepted a position as a solo librarian in Ashland and he was working in Columbus—and flying in to see me every weekend), he said, "While you are out here, let's buy a ring." Which we did. At the jewelry store, I said that I wouldn't put on the ring without a proposal, which I got: "You will marry me, won't you?" We were married in August 1983.

Barbara's Story

In 1961 I was working as a clerk in the Syracuse Public Library in Syracuse, New York. A young man, John, was working as a page while he pursued his master's degree at Syracuse University. All the women thought he was so nice but I was dating someone at the time. I remember thinking how nice he was but that he needed a woman in his life because he wore baggy pants and plaids with stripes. After I broke up with my boyfriend, a lovely librarian I worked with decided to play matchmaker and fixed us up. It was love at first date for him but took me a little longer. We were engaged after three months and married after seven months. We will celebrate our forty-second anniversary in November.

He retired after thirty-five years in social work and I retired in 2000 after ten years as a librarian assistant at Liverpool Public Library in Liverpool, New York.

I can still say he is a wonderful guy and also dresses very well.

Margo's Story

In 1996 I was working at the Rantoul Public Library as a shelver, while finishing up my bachelor's degree at the University of Illinois at Urbana-Champaign. At the library was a recently hired children's librarian, Janet Robinson. We became friends, but weren't super close.

I was very surprised one day when she asked me if I was seeing anybody. I told her not really (I had been sporadically dating a guy for four years). That was when she fixed me up on a blind date with my now husband, Tim.

Tim and I arranged our date on the phone and it was to take place at 5:30 p.m. on August 28, 1996: he was to come pick me up, we would go out to dinner, and we'd see a movie. The appointed time arrived, and he didn't show up. It was a good half hour before he arrived. He had missed the exit off of the interstate, and had to go another ten miles before he could turn back. We ended up going out to dinner (he in his shorts and Bulls T-shirt, I in my dress!) and then proceeded to go to the drive-in movie, thirty miles away. What we failed to find out was that the drive-in wasn't open during the week.

We decided to drive to the surrounding towns to find a movie we could see. I think Tim ended up driving over a hundred miles that night! We ended up seeing a movie in Champaign.

It was after the first date with Tim that night that I realized that God was directing me to him in marriage. Four years prior, in my early college days, before the first day of my class had started, I had an unearthly episode happen where I heard voices in my head scream out, "Marriage, marriage, marriage" (and believe me, I am not a person that usually hears voices in my head). I had just met a man from my class that day, and I thought the message was meant for him to be my future spouse. I was wrong. Four years later, exactly at the same day and time, I met Tim—half an hour late for our date.

Several dates later, Tim and I were talking about where he and his family lived. I not only found out that I had worked with his younger sister at a restaurant in Champaign some ten years earlier, but that I had visited their house once, but never met him.

Tim and I were married on May 31, 1997, and have three small children. God has blessed us immensely.

Annalise's Story

Nick's mother was the librarian for the district, and she hired me as a library assistant. Nick went from someone who was never in a library to someone who could never get away! After some late nights at the library shelving together (and some nagging from the other librarians!) we've been together for over two years.

Barbara's Story

I manage a small medical library and therefore space is at a premium, so I decided a huge housekeeping task was long overdue. In order to do this as quickly, inexpensively, and effortlessly (on my part!) as possible, I asked my twenty-four-year-old son Matt if he would come and give me a hand with the lifting and chucking out side of the operation. He readily agreed after a bribe of free lunch was offered and the realization that he would pick up lots of brownie points with me for the future.

The day arrived and we were busily filling plastic sacks with elderly, superseded medical tomes and "why did I keep this in the first place?" freebie journals, etc., when in walked a lovely young colleague and friend of mine to do some research. I introduced her to Matt and carried on with my task while Jenny did what she had come to do and went back to her office.

Two days later I bumped into her and she said that Matt was nice . . . who was he? When I told her she became a little embarrassed—until I told her that he had said he liked her too. Unfortunately she had a steady boyfriend at that time, so that seemed to be the end of the matter. But three months later that relationship ended and to cheer her up we went to the circus together on a Wednesday. I invited her to my house for coffee at the end of the evening and lo and behold, my son was home by then. They started talking and never stopped—before she left he had taken her phone number and they dated on the next Friday night.

That was eight years ago and they are living happily together, but we still laugh about the venue in which they met.

Fran's Story

We knew each other by sight: His girlfriend had gone to college and met someone new. My boyfriend of the time needed to return his library books before he left town (and he didn't intend to come back). He was coming out of the library. I introduced him to my soon-todepart boyfriend and chatted while my boyfriend returned his books. We married a year later and have been married now for twenty-three years.

Allan's Story

My wife and I originally met through mutual friends one evening. I immediately thought, "This is the one," but I'm a very quiet shy guy. I had just moved on from a small Christian liberal arts college in Alberta to the big university, both in Edmonton. For some reason I constantly found a reason to be where this charming woman worked, in the library at the school I had just left. We would talk and have fun with lots of friends around, but I never could get up the courage to ask her out, because I never really knew if the feeling was mutual. She got so frustrated that she talked to my roommates, who then talked to me. I was at the library that very next morning at 8:00 a.m. We recently celebrated our fifteenth anniversary!

The chief librarian at the college gave me my first library job shortly afterward, and I've been happily working in libraries ever since.

Romance @ Your Library—Prapti Mehta

Every locality in India has a corner "library," which houses the latest magazines, romances, and the top ten on the *New York Times* best-seller list. These libraries are small shacks run by entrepreneurs and usually open in the evening when everyone is back from school, university, or work. Their clientele is comprised of housewives thirsty for Bollywood gossip, teenage girls wanting to read the latest Mills and Boon romances, and teenage boys hanging around hoping to catch the eye of one of the girls frequenting the library.

My husband Anil and I met at one of these shacks all those years ago. We both lived in Hyderabad, India, at the time and our "library" was run by Bashir Bhai, who had set up his book shack in the corner of a gas station. It was a small library with enough room for only two or three people to comfortably browse through the collection of books and magazines. Anil used to go there everyday to pick up magazines for his sisters and mother and also to hang around with his friend, the owner of the gas station. My sister used to go there to pick up the latest Mills and Boon (M&B).

Anil and my sister, Trupti, were good friends. He mentored her through her many crises—usually involving her boyfriends. I first met Anil at the library. I learned later that my sister, who despaired of my ever getting a boyfriend, had orchestrated this meeting. I had gone there to pick up yet another M&B for Trupti when Anil came up to me and said, "Hello, are you Trupti's sister?" We got talking—about books naturally—and found that there were many books in common that we both loved.

I am a shy, very serious person and love reading. I found that Anil too enjoyed authors like Richard Bach, Khalil Gibran, and Ayn Rand. His favorite shop, like mine, was AA Hussain—the only bookstore that Hyderabad had in the seventies and eighties. He, like me, would spend all his pocket money there.

We talked and talked and talked a lot that day and decided to meet again the next day at the library. We were both seventeen. Over the next few years we started meeting there every day and would sit with Anil's friend in the gas station, talking about books, philosophy, art, music, and drama. I think we fell in love then.

The most exciting thing that happened to us was when the British Library opened in Hyderabad. Membership was restricted to two hundred people who had to go through a stringent assessment process. We queued up for hours to get a membership form and the happiest day of our young lives was when we were both accepted as members. From then on, we started meeting at the British Library. Poor old Bashir Bhai could never understand why we preferred this library to his wooden shack!

Anil and I married on October 26, 1983. We now live in Perth, Australia. We have two children who share our love for books. Very often, Anil calls up from work and says, "Shall we meet at the library tonight?" We meet there with the kids and spend hours there.

My sisters and brother still cannot understand how anyone could fall in love in a library. It is difficult to explain to someone who does not love books as much as we do.

Note

1. Pseudonym.

CHAPTER SIXTEEN

If Food Be the Music of Romance

Food has always played a prominent role in romance. It also plays a prominent role in a library context. Librarians produce cookbooks, they hold extravagant potluck dinners, and they enjoy socializing over meals, wine, and coffee. Library staff rooms groan with home baking at the holidays. My own staff room is graced annually by a splendid array of homemade chocolates, thanks to the special talent of our head of acquisitions.

My first day at library school gave me a hunch that librarians have a romance with food. The teaching staff was giving us an orientation to the program, the building, and the campus. We were all getting bored. One of the younger staff announced she was going to tell us about food and where to get it. I can still hear in my mind the way she enunciated the word "food" many times in the course of her presentation—like a sustained note of music. Her audience listened keenly, with renewed interest.

Margy, a former colleague—and an excellent cook—introduced me to her surefire lasagna some years ago. I was at that heady stage when a friend suddenly seemed to be moving into the realm of romantic partner. I had invited him for dinner, and was seeking Margy's advice on a menu. She assured me that her lasagna recipe was sure to lead to a marriage proposal, as it had in her own case. I was comfortably single, and marriage was certainly not on my agenda. However, I couldn't resist the challenge and decided to make the lasagna. Margy knew what she was talking about: a marriage proposal indeed ensued after the dishes were washed (he helped). We went from first kiss to engagement in six days. I have included Margy's recipe in an appendix—which seems an appropriate place for it. Make it with extreme care, and only if you are prepared for the possible consequences.

Margy and her librarian husband met in the very first week of library school during a library tour. In her words, one week later he walked her home and after sampling her cooking, they were soon dating. One week after that he proposed. They married after graduation and celebrated their eighteenth anniversary in 2004.

Margy is known for her puns. When I asked her what she thought was the key to an enduring library romance she replied, "The real secret is to be unshelfish with each other."

Only Good Things Happen in the Library—Maria Coletta McLean (For Bob)

I was on my way to the Weston library when I met Bob. He was coming out of the bank, just about to jump into his Chevy II convertible, when my friend called out to him. When she introduced us I felt a ping in my chest, felt my face grow flushed. I noticed the deep tan, the sunglasses, the preppy clothes, and the gold signet ring. It was just a quick hello and he jumped into his convertible and pulled onto Main Street.

"He just broke up with his girlfriend," said my friend. "Cute, huh?"

Yes, definitely cute but completely out of my league. From his tan and sun-bleached hair I imagined he spent a lot of time just driving around in that convertible. All the rest of the way to the library I imagined myself riding beside him.

The following day when I arrived at the library, Bob just happened to be sitting at the oak table reading the newspaper. The light streaming through the leaded library windows was shining on him like a spotlight. I set up my schoolbooks in my usual spot; I was in my last year of high school, studying for finals but that day I studied Bob. He was reading the business section of *The Globe and Mail*. I thought of *The Globe* as a newspaper for businesspeople or rich people or . . . well, not for ordinary people.

An hour later when I was gathering my books Bob happened to be leaving too and we walked out together. "Where do you live?" he asked. "Can I give you a lift?"

My mother didn't like convertibles. She believed all that wind gave you sore throats, stiff necks, and a host of other ailments. There was no way I could show up in a convertible with a boy she'd never met and expect to get away with it. I wasn't at all sure I could explain this to Bob. He was a confident middle-class young man and I was the shy seventeen-year-old daughter of immigrant parents with old-fashioned ideas. The only thing we had in common was the library.

"I can walk. Thanks anyway."

"Wait a minute. There's a dance at the church on Saturday night. I thought you might like to go with me. I could pick you up."

By now we were standing beside his car. "Wait a minute," he said again and he unhooked the roof and gave it a backward push. The roof folded neatly into itself with a sigh. I sighed too, thinking of how to explain my mother's convertible phobia. And I'd have to ask him which church was hosting the dance. Then I'd have to admit my mother's insistence on meeting every friend and her crazy idea that I must be home by midnight. If Bob was still interested in taking me to the dance, I'd have to tell my mother that Bob probably wasn't Catholic and he certainly wasn't Italian.

"My mother's not too fond of convertibles," I began.

"My grandmother's like that," said Bob. "When I bought it I wanted her to be the first person to have a ride in it. Even though it was October I put down the roof and she put on her winter coat and her winter hat and off we went."

"How'd she like it?"

"When I assured her that the car was on sale and I'd paid cash, she liked it fine."

A man who paid cash for his car—my dad was sure to like Bob. Mom was going to be harder. Of course it might be cool enough on Saturday night to keep the roof up. With luck it could rain.

"Okay," I said all in a rush. "I need to ask my parents. And they'll want to meet you. And I have to be home by midnight. And which church is holding the dance?"

"Central United. Does it matter?"

"Not really. It's just that I'm Catholic and. . . . Not really."

So I told my mother I'd met Bob at the library and that he was a friend of a friend. The library setting gave the whole meeting a sense of respectability. Over the years I'd spent a lot of time in the library and nothing bad had ever happened there so I think my mother thought of it as a safe place. For me it was peaceful and protected. I'd had polio as a child and it had left me unable to play and run as tirelessly as other children. I compensated by replacing sports with reading, the gym with the library. Good things happened at the library so my mother would associate Bob with a good place.

"I don't want my daughter riding around in a car with no roof."

"I'll keep the roof up, Mrs. Coletta."

"And she has to be home by midnight."

"I'll make sure, Mrs. Coletta."

"The dance is at the church?"

"Yes, Mrs. Coletta. Right in the church hall."

"Okay. Have a good time. Don't forget. Home by midnight."

"Yes, thanks, Mrs. Coletta."

"Sorry about that," I said to Bob. "My parents are old-fashioned and over-protective and. . . ."

"They're fine."

As it turned out, Bob turned out to be pretty fine as well. We were nothing alike and yet I liked everything about him. It started with the dance. When it was over, at eleven o'clock, a group of friends were going to Bob's parents' house for a drink. I didn't drink and as I said my mother wanted me home before midnight, but I got in the car with the others rather than admit my unreasonable curfew.

No one was home at Bob's house but there were snacks set out in the recreation room. Behind the bar was a large mirror lined with liquor bottles of every kind on glass shelves; beneath the bar were a sink and a little fridge. The room was like something out of a movie. The basements I knew had sausages and bunches of herbs hanging from the ceiling and demijohns of homemade wine fermenting between shelves laden with canned tomatoes.

Bob mixed drinks that I'd never heard of for everyone: sloe gin and ginger ale, whiskey sour, Adams on ice (my family only drank wine: red or white); he poured ginger ale for himself. Okay, I said to myself. He's not so different. I know what ginger ale is. But it was Vernor's Ginger

Ale, a brand I'd never heard of. Someone put some Buddy Holly on the record player, couples danced, someone phoned for pizza, no one looked at the clock. At exactly eleven forty-five, Bob took me into the hallway and opened the closet door to get my coat. "Got to get you home by midnight," he said with a smile. The light went on in the closet: the light went on in my head: this was the one.

"Want to go out tomorrow?" he asked.

"Tomorrow's Sunday," I reminded him but no light went on in his head. "I have to spend Sunday with my family. Don't you?"

"With my family?" Bob repeated. Completely baffled. Like I was from another planet—a nice planet, friendly, kind but definitely kind of odd.

"I can't go out on Sunday," I said. "Would you like to come to my house for dinner?"

He brought flowers for my mother. We didn't have a vase; my aunt had to go downstairs to her place and find something and there was a big discussion about whether or not to cut the ends off the flowers or just put them in the way they were. While that debate was going on in the kitchen, I took Bob into the living room and introduced him around: my dad, my brother, my sister-in-law, my nephew, my sister, my sister's boyfriend, my cousins. . . . Partway around the room we had to detour around the dining room table, which had been pulled out to its full length and protruded into the living room like a small peninsula. Bob started to look uncomfortable. I said, "Don't worry. You don't have to remember everyone's name." He said, "But who are all these people?" "Just family. Mostly cousins." "Are these all your cousins?" he asked—and he looked serious, as if I might have invited my whole family to dinner just to meet him.

"Of course not. These cousins just dropped in on their way up north. Usually there's only about a dozen of us for dinner. Tonight's a bit of an exception." I asked him about his cousins. He said he had three. I said I had about thirty-three.

Most of the dinner conversation centered on counting cousins—did we have thirty-three or more?—and that led to heated discussions about cousins living in Italy and the States and whether we were including them in the count. Next there was a secondary debate about first cousins and second cousins compared to cousins-once-removed. What was a cousin-once-removed anyway?

We ate my mother's homemade ravioli and drank Uncle Primo's homemade wine. The meatballs sparked a second lively discussion between my two aunts regarding the addition of ground pork and veal and whether the extra expense was worth it. A third debate took off from there concerning parmesan cheese—should it be added to the meatballs before cooking or just sprinkled on afterwards? Then I brought in the salad and my brother taught Bob his "secret method" of cutting a meatball in half and wiping the spaghetti sauce off his plate with the meatball half so that the plate was cleaned for the salad. The salad dressing was made with oil and my Uncle Primo's wine from last year that had turned to vinegar. Bob was asking why we ate our salad after our meal and what were these dark leaves (dandelions), and he missed most of the argument about who made the best wine in the family. A little later my brother taught Bob his second secret method of stirring the sugar into his coffee and then quickly adding the milk so you could do two additions in one stir. That led to my uncle telling a story about one time when they went fishing with Uncle Mario and . . . I realized that Bob had given up on trying to keep up with the conversation and was sitting back, just like my dad, letting the voices and the laughter swirl around him.

I went to his house for dinner the following week. We sat in the living room, amongst freshly polished end tables adorned with starched lace doilies and vases of porcelain flowers. To get to the couch I had to walk across an Indian carpet with visible vacuum marks and see my footsteps once I sat down. Bob's parents asked me where we'd met and I told them about the library. Then they asked about school and I started talking about *Wuthering Heights*. I thought it was going pretty well until I realized they were talking about a movie ("There's a movie?") and I was talking about the book ("There's a book?").

First we had iceberg lettuce quarters in individual wooden bowls. There were bottles of salad dressing on the table and I got very tense trying to choose one. Blue cheese, Thousand Island, and ranch: I'd never heard of these dressings. Then Bob's father asked me how I liked my roast beef and I said, "Fine," and Bob said, "He means, do you like it rare or well-done?" I blushed rare and said, "Well done, please."

Then Bob's father offered me horseradish (what on earth is horserad-ish?) and Bob's mother offered me sour cream for my baked potato (sour cream?). After that, no one spoke; they just ate. I got so unnerved by the silence that I forgot to eat my foil-wrapped baked potato waiting in its own little wicker basket to the left of my plate. "Did you not like your potato?" asked Bob's mother. I assured her I had just overlooked it and they sat and politely waited while I ate my potato. Sweat gath-ered under my armpits and erupted across my forehead, as I forked pieces of a potato the size of P.E.I.[1] into my mouth. For dessert we had a store-bought pie: apple. Bob's mother cut the pie in quarters and started putting it on the dessert plates. I was trying to think of a polite way to say I couldn't eat a quarter of a pie and Bob's father was offering me cream for my coffee so I said no, thank you. I was left to choke down bitter black coffee while they ate their pie. We had a little con-versation with our dessert. Bob's parents said they'd gone to a restau-rant in Buffalo for Sunday dinner (who drives to Buffalo for Sunday dinner?) with some friends (Sunday dinner with friends!) and as they were ordering their dessert they saw a waiter go by carrying a large plate in front of him. "It was like a silver cake pedestal," Bob's mother said. They said they'd asked the waiter what he was serving—it smelled so delicious—and the waiter had said, "Pizza pie." They were so intrigued with this new type of pie that they ordered one for dessert. "It tasted great," they said.

"It's an Italian dish. Do you know it? Pizza pie." I didn't know what to say. I felt this dinner was like the Last Supper; our worlds were too different.

We were on our way to the library—I was telling Bob about a char-acter in a book, *A Tree Grows in Brooklyn*, who was trying to read her way alphabetically through the library. "I had that same idea when I was a little girl," I said, "before we moved to Weston. The bookmobile used to come to our school in Humber Summit and with only two walls of books it seemed possible to read them all."

Bob was telling me about a merger between two grocery chains and how that would affect pricing. He was carrying my schoolbooks; when we got to the library I'd study and he'd read the business magazines or *The Globe*. Inside the library our worlds didn't seem so impossibly far apart but outside, in the real world, I wasn't sure how we could create a future out of such differences.

An elderly couple came walking along and Bob pointed them out to me. They were well into their seventies. The man carried a newspaper under his arm and the woman had a book and they were talking softly to each other. He said, "That's how I want to be when I'm old, walking along enjoying the day and still holding hands with my wife."

We were married seven months later. Everyone said we were too young and too different. Still we had those two things going for us: we'd met at the library where only good things happen and we'd seen our future in that older couple walking along holding hands.

Susan's Story

I began working in a small public library in northeastern Pennsylvania in 1998. We had a patron, Jack, who was in once or twice per week to use the microfilm as he was building a local genealogy research database. The four other employees knew him, but they didn't know that I didn't know anything about this nice-looking man. We took notice of one another but assumed each other must be "taken" based on our ages (I'm now forty-three and he's fifty).

Finally, in early March 2002, while he was chatting with two of us at the desk one day it somehow came out in the conversation that neither of us had ever been married nor were we in current relationships. A coworker and I stopped by his house the day of our local St. Patrick's Day parade (actually, she insisted I had to go in) and met some of his relatives. That night I e-mailed my thanks for his hospitality. We began e-mailing daily and finding out a lot about each other as well as chatting more in the library. Then, in late March, he asked me if I liked lasagna and offered to make dinner for me. I went over to his house the next night and we talked for hours. We've been together ever since and were married October 12, 2002. He has done so much local history and genealogical research he is the main resource patrons can contact if they want local genealogy information. As I still work in this library, I often joke that people doing research now get "two-for-one" when they need help. If I can't help them I just pick up the phone and call him and let him help them. We couldn't be happier!

My husband reminded me of the two songs that come to mind when we think of our first dates: "Feels Like Home" (Van Morrison) and "So Quiet in Here" (Linda Ronstadt). I now see that title is a bit ironic for a book about libraries.

Ruth's Story

I moved from Canada to Arkansas in 1996 to work at the Saline County Libraries as their children's services librarian. Jessie Cranford was then branch manager of the library in Bryant. She adopted me into her family. She changed jobs to go work at the University of Arkansas at Little Rock School of Law. She held casual parties for library employees. I attended a few. I was going to skip one when our mutual friend Greta called me to come save her from being the only non–law school library person there. She called me twice in ten minutes. For my friend, I went. We played card games, ate food, and had fun and apparently Steve Hyatt was flirting madly and directing it at me. I was totally clueless. A week later he called me for dinner. I had just been flattened by two separate crushes and didn't want to date but thought what the hell—I deserve a dinner and he's a nice guy. So, I went. We ate Italian food, went for coffee (which I don't drink—the date must have been going well), and then went for a long, long drive. Not one of my chimes of suburban paranoia went off and we even saw a shooting star! Four months later we were engaged—you cannot deny celestial pyrotechnics. Nine months after that we were married, and eleven months after that we had our first child. I was pregnant when I finally walked down the aisle with my father at our second wedding in Canada.

Stephanie's Story

It was my second day at work in my first librarian job in a public library in Melbourne, Australia. Ross had also just started work at the same time; I remember opening the staff door to him and saying hi to him for the first time. I liked him, but another colleague was very flirtatious with him and I didn't want to compete for his intentions!

About six months after we started, we were working together quite closely. He asked me out for a drink after work. As there was no bars nearby I suggested I cook dinner for him.

We talked until midnight, when he left. Before he left he gave me the softest kiss goodnight. We went out, got married, and our first child is due in March 2005.

Cathie's Story

I was manning a small branch library when my future husband staggered in a little worse for wear (he'd been imbibing) and demanded to know why the library had sent him such a rude letter! We did in those days (thirty years ago) threaten all sorts of things if books weren't returned on time. It transpired he'd left the book in a seaman's mission in Australia and he ended up inviting me out for a meal. This turned out to be a large drink and a small but tasty pork pie! Happy days!

Valerie's Story

I met my husband, Bill, at the British Columbia Courthouse Society Library, in 1992, where we both worked. I am a librarian and was switching from a reference librarian position to be head of technical services. At this time he had just started as the library's accountant. We ended up very close in terms of office proximity, and over the course of a couple of years, discovered we were the only ones who worked late in the evenings and came in on weekends. The accountant was a quiet fellow, new to Vancouver, and the most that anyone had found out about him was he loved chocolate and was studying for his CGA designation. After almost four years had passed, I came back to work after lunch one day to find a beautiful bag of jelly beans on my desk. No one confessed to leaving them there, so I was left wondering.

One evening shortly after that when we were both working late, we got talking about baseball and the next thing you know we were set to go to a baseball game together. That was the end of August 1996, and we were married on December 28, 1996. I don't remember any particular music or song associated with our romance, but I sure remember the chocolate. It was, of course, the accountant who had left the jelly beans. He told me later he had had his eye on me for quite a while, but wasn't sure he wanted to work in the same place as someone he was seeing, so he had been thinking about taking a job somewhere else. Once we were married, he was a little uncomfortable with both of us working at the same place, so he took a job a couple of years later with a property management firm, and I was left to forge on at the library. No one knew about our romance until we told the director and then the staff. It was quite a surprise to everyone! He did get his CGA designation and has since changed firms. We are still happily married.

Note

1. P.E.I., or Prince Edward Island, is famous for its potato industry.

CHAPTER SEVENTEEN

Miscellanea

A number of stories were hard to classify, but all have something to say about the power of libraries. In each one there is a sense of a library playing an important emotional role in the subject's experience, whether it's a redemptive or a developmental one. The effect is often profound and transformational.

Libraries can be the source of enduring friendships. Bill Richardson, Canadian writer, broadcaster, and humorist was for a while a children's librarian at the Kelowna Library in British Columbia. He brought ingenuity and madcap humor to his puppet shows and other programs, with scripts full of subtext that appealed to child and adult alike. Many local mothers would make a point of taking their children to Bill's programs, ostensibly for their children; but in the process they enjoyed not only Bill's creative genius but also made lasting friendships with one another in the process. Library lovers tend to ensure their children inherit their love of libraries and reading.

Spring Lea's Story

In 1990, I was a freshman going to Adams State College in Alamosa, Colorado, where I met a guy named Ray while playing Dungeons & Dragons with some friends. The attraction for me was immediate, but not for him. He told me that he just didn't think of me "that way." But I was nothing if not tenacious. While I didn't want to force the issue with him, I thought perhaps that by remaining within his sight and proving over and over again what a good friend I could be, then maybe someday that persistence might win out and a romance could blossom. So, I started dogging him around school, even taking computer classes just to be near him. Within weeks, my interest in computers became real, and I set myself up with a minor in computer science.

Flash forward four years to life after college. Ray and I are still just friends, I'm still in Alamosa, and I'm working a retail job I hate. Wanting something more out of life, I started scouting for jobs, which included polishing my résumé. This meant making a trip to my local public library for a book on the subject and discovering in the process that they had an opening for a technical services assistant. After landing the job, I found out that it was my impressive computer skills (in addition to my degree in English/psychology) that helped me edge out the competition.

After working there for three years, I decided that getting an MLS would be a very good idea. I applied for and gained admittance to Emporia State University's School of Library and Information Management program in Denver. By that time, Ray, who was still my good friend, was living in Colorado Springs, which was a nice stopping point for my biweekly commute from Alamosa to Denver for graduate school. I managed to have dinner with him several times over the three years of classes.

While earning my degree, I accomplished quite a bit of networking in Colorado library land and had pretty much decided paradise was to be found in Castle Rock, a rapidly growing township just south of metro Denver. The library district in Douglas County seemed to be a perfect match for my philosophy of patron service, and I thought they could benefit from the services of an up-and-coming librarian who was very eager to work with teens. I guess they thought so, too, because I was hired within four months of graduating with my MLS.

Castle Rock, as it turns out, is only forty-one miles from Ray's house in Colorado Springs, which really isn't all that much when the speed limit is seventy-five miles per hour on the interstate. Over the next two years, we started seeing a lot more of each other: going to the Renaissance Festival; going to movies together; having dinner and parties at each other's homes. And we augmented these visits with far more e-mail than we had ever written in the previous decade.

Finally, twelve years after we first laid eyes on each other, Ray fell in love with me and I with him. When I mentioned to Ray that following him to all those computer classes was what led me to get my MLS, he was the one who pointed out that getting my MLS was what led me back to him, something that made me feel fated to be with him. We two soul mates were wed on June 21, 2004, the summer solstice, because, as Ray pointed out, getting married on the longest day of the year will promote a long marriage. It just goes to show that true love will prevail in the end . . . even if it takes fourteen years and an MLS to figure it all out.

Anita's[2] Story

Three years ago, I fell deeply in love with a wonderful woman named Martha. When informing her mother that she had a new relationship, Martha told her the things about me she knew her mother would want to know and would approve of: "She has beautiful hazel eyes, Ma, and we met in church . . . and oh yeah, she's a librarian." According to Martha, "That was all she needed to hear." I was in like Flynn . . . her mother knows librarians can do no wrong!

Margaret's Story

It was a toddler storytime at the downtown library on a winter Sunday afternoon—another mother and I got chatting. The children were grown up long ago; we now live on different continents, correspond intermittently (even in these days of e-mail), and meet only every five years or so, but when we do it's as though not a week has passed since the last meeting.

Judith's Story

I met my husband at doggie playgroup, love at first sight: he for my dog, I for him! Then he looked up and saw me, so it was love at second sight for him. Bessey and I (then a library student at the Palmer School Long Island University, Brookville, New York) moved in with Jeff and Net-oot the following week and got pregnant with Olivia Rose. I was hired when I was six months pregnant on the day before Halloween at the East Williston Library, and in February "the library baby" was born. Today, the library baby is now a voracious reader at seven years old, and Netoot and Bessey are her favorite audience.

Judy's Story

My love for libraries is not a romantic one, but I have loved them most of my life. I had never been in one until I started school and was introduced to the school library. I grew up very poor in the rural South and should probably have fit into the ignorant (or uneducated) stereotype but books proved to be my salvation. There was no kindergarten, head start program, or prekindergarten back then. I thought books were a miracle and I still do.

As soon as I could put a few words together, I started reading and haven't stopped since. I can remember that the school librarian wouldn't let me check out *Nancy Drew* books when I was in third grade because she thought I was too young. Instead, I read my sister's when she brought them home. We lived several miles out in the country with limited transportation so it was difficult to get to the library and return books on time. I thought the summer bookmobile was wonderful. The driver soon learned that I was responsible and would allow me to borrow more books than she normally did.

I am fifty-eight now and I still remember her name after all these years. Talk about impressions! Her name was Iris Sikes. She lived in Coffee County, Georgia, where I also grew up. I am sure she is deceased now, but I still have very fond memories of her kindness to me.

I read to my children and now my daughter is keeping up the tradition. She has a master's in library science. I did not get to go to college until after she started in 1993. I enrolled for my undergrad in 1994 and now I too have my master's in library science. I earned it two years ago from Florida State University. I only wish I had been able to do so forty years ago but I am still very proud of it.

Dorothy's Story

This story is written by someone born in 1910, hence the old-fashioned descriptions. It is set in the village of Richmond Hill, Ontario, in which I lived from the age of four or five until further education took me to the metropolis. Our only place for entertainment, other than the churches' Sunday schools, was the Masonic Hall at the back of which, reached by a separate entrance, was a large square room with bookshelves along three sides. This constituted our town library. The library was open Wednesday evening and Saturday afternoon.

I had a brother only sixteen months older than myself and we were both prodigious readers as well as being physically active. But radios were just coming into homes gradually and my mother was a young widow, so we couldn't afford such luxuries. We had a crystal set which we put together from a kit and if we fiddled with it long enough we would get scratchy sounds and eventually "CKEY Schenectady" and usually a musical show and sometimes vaudeville or drama. The drawback with this was we had to use earphones so only one person could listen at a time and with our scrungy little set it would often conk out and had to be tuned in all over again. Hence we did a great deal of reading which took us to the library on Wednesday evenings and Saturday afternoons, the brother always looking after the little sister, since he was required to be the "man" of our home.

The librarian was a gentleman called Mr. Phipps. He was probably forty or so but we considered him elderly. He was a very stately gentleman of medium height, a little bit square but not fat. He had white hair, was slightly bald, and had a very neat, well-kept "goatee," and a nice complexion, and was very well dressed with a coat, vest, and tie.

We traveled by the radial street car. The commuting took an hour to the city limits, where another street car took us to just above the old train station. My brother and I would be selecting books and trying to discuss them quietly and Mr. Phipps was always putting his fingers to his lips and making ssshh, ssshh sounds which caused us to get the giggles and then we would try to get our books registered and out of there as soon as possible. This situation was an inevitable happening every time we went; I think it probably amused Mr. Phipps too but his position would not allow him to show it.

Keith's Story

My parents, Elspeth and Doug Walker, met at the University of Saskatchewan Library in 1945 and from then on "library" seemed to get into the blood of the family as eventually almost all six of us worked in libraries. But their start in the university library doesn't really have the markings of a budding romance. She wrote about their first encounter in her autobiography: "I recall this serious, and if the truth be known, rather grumpy-appearing young (not bad looking!) guy, sitting in the university library, often glowering at these flibbertigibbet freshwomen who looked up from their texts every time a guy came in, and whose giggling and lack of academic zeal must have driven this seasoned, serious student up the wall!" Soon, however, they were in love and got married on a Wednesday evening because "Wednesdays were 'half-day holidays' in Saskatoon so the Library [by that time my mom was in charge of the West Side Branch of Saskatoon Public Library] was closed and my friends could attend the wedding."

Katie's Story

Before I decided to become a librarian, I used to be a nurse, and spent all my spare time in my local public library. One Friday afternoon, I noticed a gorgeous long-haired student-looking guy at the next public workstation. He wasn't looking at his screen—he was looking at me! But he quickly looked away when I spotted him. I was equally coy, and smiled in his general direction before looking back at my screen and trying to sneak glances in his direction from beneath my hair. Suddenly, he was gone—I looked around—he wasn't at the circulation desk, he didn't seem to be among the shelves—he had disappeared.

The next Friday afternoon, I happened to be in the library again: I walked into the library straight past him as he walked out. I watched him go.

I figured Fridays were the days to be in the library. Thus began a complicated pattern of trying to ensure that I got an early shift at work so I could take a slow walk down to the library, and spend the afternoon in there, waiting.

He was there again a few weeks later—back at the online catalog. I couldn't resist a peek at his searches: Greek literature, Euripides, Medea. I learned to hang around in the literature section, and started to read some of the same kinds of books. It made a change from reading feminist literature.

A few weeks later, it paid off, and we got chatting (quietly) about the joys of Greek tragedies. He learned to find me in the music section (discovering Stina Nordenstam) and it became a regular, unspoken date. We'd casually find each other hidden among the shelves, spend a few hours reading together, swapping titles and CD suggestions, and just talking.

Then one day, as usual, I turned up to the library. I was there until closing time, but he never appeared. The same thing happened the following week. And the week after that. I never saw him again.

I loved our encounters. I never knew his name, I didn't know where he lived, and there were no promises, or commitments, or even sneaky kisses hidden in the stacks. But I did go on to study Greek drama at the Open University before studying to qualify as a librarian. I hope, somewhere in his collection, he has a Stina Nordenstam CD. And a library card.

Michelle's Story[4]

The library saved my life.

My abusive relationship turned sour when it escalated into violence. He abused me physically, mentally, and sexually. I lost all my friends and became the perfect stereotype of an abused woman. I dressed ugly and did nothing but sit around with my boyfriend. I was surprised that the library would hire me, looking the way I did, like a freaky punk girl who was afraid to talk to anyone at all. My first employee progress report said that I was "pretty quiet."

I started reading about abuse; the more I read the more I realized that if I didn't do something soon I could end up seriously injured or worse, dead. Finally I had enough of it; my boyfriend had recently cheated on me and then had kicked me in the ribs with his steel toe boots. I decided to break up with him.

This was easier said than done; if I hadn't have been working at the library I probably would still be with him. I started talking to people and thinking that maybe I wasn't such a bad-looking girl, that maybe I had a future after all. When I broke up with my boyfriend, he freaked out, and I was scared for my life. I got threatening phone calls and visits from him. But I held out, and didn't get back together with him no matter how much I hurt inside.

My coworkers don't know this, but they saved my life, by being so accepting and nice to me. I found a sanctuary at the library. When I told my parents about the abuse they wanted me to go to counseling, and I did for a couple of weeks, but the real help came from people like the employees at the library. I was with my boyfriend for a total of three and a half years, and within the first month of working at the library I was independent and free again. I am proud to say that this was over two years ago now, and I am a new person, I talk constantly and I even think that sometimes my coworkers would like me to just shut up already! I just want to let people know that just being kind can impact someone's life so much, and I decided a long time ago that I will always have faith in people.

Notes

1. Pseudonym.
2. Pseudonym.
3. Pseudonym.
4. Pseudonym.

CHAPTER EIGHTEEN

P.S.: We Love You

What are the common themes that emerge from the stories? It's noticeable that Thursday evening seems to be when a library's romantic powers are at their height. Story after story noted a couple's first encounter took place on a Thursday. Take note, those who plan library programs: Thursday singles nights at the public library could prove very popular. Libraries are largely viewed as safe, secure, and trustworthy (intellectual freedom challenges notwithstanding). Meeting someone in a library is perhaps considered less potentially dangerous than meeting someone in a bar. Prospective partners might have assumptions about a person who uses or works in a library. Several stories mention the parental approval that came with finding a romantic partner who worked at a library. When Colin Perchard, former director of the British Council Division, officiated at the fortieth anniversary celebrations for the British Council Library in Pune, India, he shared his view that the library promotes cultural activities and romance too, considering the library "a safe meeting ground."[1]

It is noticeable too, that travel frequently plays a part in the stories. Librarianship is a peripatetic profession—not just within the country but also cross-border and even internationally. Couples noted that they wouldn't have had a chance of meeting in the normal course of their lives if it weren't for library-initiated travel.

The library community can be close-knit. Librarians share their sorrows and their joys. Significant celebrations of life take place at the library. Several weddings were planned either for when the library was

closed to allow the staff to attend, or the library was officially closed to
enable the staff to be present.

Librarians pay attention to detail, as their narratives demonstrate.
Dates, times, and distances are all charted in the stories, whether the
events recalled are recent or distant.

Contrary to the depressing stereotypes of the profession which tend
to exercise us, this book shows that romantic and passionate souls are
alive and well in the library. Hearts are beating within us regardless of
the dowdy exterior the media seems determined to bestow.

Many stories refer to a love of reading as a factor that brought couples together. Some couples come from different backgrounds and cultures, brought together nevertheless in often serendipitous ways by
their common love of libraries and what they represent. What romantic couples who met in the library often refer to as fate is perhaps just
another version of the serendipity of the stacks.

While journalist Deborah Orr expresses concern about the condition of public libraries today, she calls the Carnegie Library she remembers from her childhood "an oasis of lush possibility."[2]

When Rudolfo Anaya donated his papers to the library at the University of New Mexico, he said

Nearly fifty years ago I enrolled at UNM. The building I most visited and
learned to love was Zimmerman Library. I spent countless hours here: reading, thinking, writing papers. Friends would drop by, and we took breaks to
drink coffee on the south patio or the west portal.

Here I learned to reverence books.

It's fair to say this library became my church. These reading rooms were
the nave and atrium of the adobe-stuccoed cathedral. The apse was
approached only during an epiphany which a book might offer. During those
moments of insight my eyes were suddenly opened to a new awareness, a
light I had not seen before, a glimpse of the truths I sought. The stacks were
the towers of my cathedral. Up there I was closer to the seraphims of knowledge. A carroll [sic] became my monk's cell where I read long into the night.

I was a budding writer, but I never dreamed that someday my manuscripts
would rest in this temple of learning. I was just a Chicanito from the barrio
who had not been prepared for the life of a scholar. But I fell in love with
the revelations in books. I began to write poetry. There were a few of those
black-haired beauties from northern New Mexico who hung around for me

to slip them a poem. I met my wife here, and started slipping her the poems. Poetry works. I'm still writing her poems.[3]

Ben Macintyre also picks up on the theme of library as an edifice of spiritual significance:

> I have spent a substantial portion of my life . . . in libraries, and I still enter them with a mixture of excitement and awe. I am not alone in this. Veneration for libraries is as old as writing itself, for a library is more to our culture than a collection of books: it is a temple, a symbol of power, the hushed core of civilization, the citadel of memory, with its own mystique, social and sensual as well as intellectual. Even people who never enter libraries instinctively understand their symbolic power.[4]

Macintyre goes on to expound why, in the face of massive digitization projects, the physical library will endure: "the traditional library will also survive, because a library is central to our understanding of what it is to be human."[5]

Library couples appear to be busy instilling a love of reading and libraries in their children. When two library lovers unite and produce a new generation of library lovers, should we really be worried about the demise of the library? As this love is transferred and propagated from generation to generation, is it too romantic a notion to believe the library and the values it embodies are going from strength to strength? If libraries breed romance, could romance breed libraries?

Notes

1. Chavan Shaan, "More than Words," *Indian Express*, October 1, 1999 at www.expressindia.com/morethanwords.htm (accessed August 5, 2004).

2. Deborah Orr, A *Trip to the Library Should be Inspiring*, October 26, 2004 at http://comment.independent.co.uk.?columnists_m_z/deborah_orr/story?story = 576028 (accessed January 9, 2005).

3. Rudolfo Anaya, 2004. As reported in *REFORMA Newsletter* 22, no. 2 (Summer 2004).

4. Ben Macintyre, "Paradise Is Paper, Vellum and Dust." The *Times* December 18, 2004: 24. Used with permission from NI Syndication.

5. Ibid.

Margy's Matrimonial Lasagna

To lighten this up, you can have some layers with just mozzarella and some with just béchamel.

Basic Ingredients
4 or 5 sheets of lasagna, or enough individual noodles for at least 4
   layers
hot pepper flakes/rosemary to dust the top
1 cup grated parmesan and/or Romano cheese
mozzarella: buy the rectangular slices and figure 4 slices per layer

Meat Sauce
1½ lbs. lean ground beef, cooked through and drained
2 cans crushed tomatoes
1 large can tomato paste
5 sticks celery, washed and diced
1 green and/or 1 red pepper, diced
1 onion, diced
5 cloves of garlic, diced

As much as you like of the following: red pepper flakes, oregano, basil, rosemary

Mix all of the above. Let simmer overnight to mellow the flavor.

Béchamel Sauce
½ cup butter
½ cup flour

2¹/₂ cups milk
1¹/₂ cups grated Parmesan and/or Romano cheese

As much as you like of the following: basil, oregano, rosemary, red pepper flakes, pepper

Melt the butter over medium-high heat. Stir in flour. Sauté for a minute or two. Stir in peppers and herbs. Stir for a minute or two. Stir in milk gradually, keeping the lumps out. As it starts to thicken, add the cheese. Stir well. Make sure to scrape the bottom and to give the sauce a good stir each time you add it to the lasagna.

Building the Lasagna
Preheat oven to 375 degrees Fahrenheit. Have both sauces hot and ready to go. Dip the precooked lasagna sheets in hot water, or cook noodles if using the separate ones and have them all ready to go. Coat the bottom of a lasagna pan lightly with tomato sauce, just enough to stop the first layer of noodles from sticking. Add a layer of noodles. Add layer of meat sauce. Add layer of béchamel. Add layer of mozzarella. Repeat until the pan is filled, ending on a noodle layer. Top noodles with mozzarella and grated Parmesan or Romano, then sprinkle rosemary and/or red pepper flakes on top. You can wrap it well and freeze it at this point.

Bake for 30 minutes or so. When sauce bubbles up from underneath the cheese, it should be ready. You may have to cover the top with tinfoil.

Let stand 5 minutes under foil to firm up for easier serving.